Dan LeLaCheuı
pastor needs to

MW01224156

and Dan has something vital and fresh from the heart of God. The biblical practice of pronouncing a blessing on the next generation will bring health and healing to your family and light a torch in the church. In fact, it is quite possible *The Legacy Lives On* will reverse the nightmarish statistic reminding us that most Christian youth depart from the faith and abandon their biblical roots when they leave for college. Tears of love, pride, and hope engulfed my wife and me as we blessed our son and marked his passage from childhood to manhood. None of us has been the same since. Read and embrace this revelation from God. It will start a revival in your family and a revolution in the church.

Jeff Farmer
President, Open Bible Churches
Des Moines, Iowa

Of all of the ministry that I have encountered in my twenty years of ministry to families, none has been more significant than the Blessing Ceremony of the laying on of hands of parents upon their children. Dan LeLaCheur has rediscovered a wonderful Key to the Kingdom which powerfully transfers God's blessing to young people through the significant words and touch of their parents. Our church has had several Blessing Ceremonies and numerous families have experienced the impact of generational blessing imparted from fathers and mothers to sons and daughters. God has ordained this powerful means of transferal, and you must discover this key for your own church and family!

Pastor Tom Rupli
Pastor of New Life Tabernacle
Petersburg, Michigan

The sixth grade Blessing provided us with a real intentional way of communicating our blessings to our daughter. The entire process, including the classes Chelsea attended, the letters her relatives wrote, creating her display, and preparing for the celebration, gave new meaning to the time when our daughter would pass from childhood into young adulthood. We look back on the blessing as a significant moment in her life.

Judy and Kelly Kight
Parents of Chelsea, a sixth grader
who was blessed
Spokane, Washington

One of the vital transitions in every person's life is that critical jump from grade school to junior high. It is a time of dramatic changes—emotionally, physically, socially, and spiritually.

As a pastor, I was concerned about how many of our young people were dropping out of church right after sixth grade, and we determined to do what we could to help them and their parents negotiate all the rapids that come with this important transition. One of the key elements of our efforts was "The Sixth Grade Blessing"—a very special event where our graduating sixth graders verbally express their goals and dreams for their future, and where their parents speak words of blessing over them. It's a life-changing experience for everyone, and the number of young people who drop out of church has greatly decreased.

I have found that success in life comes down to how well you handle these transition; the sixth grade blessing has been a wonderful tool to help young people and their families.

Pastor Monte J. LeLaCheur
First Church of the Open Bible
Spokane, Washington

It is my deepest honor to lift up Pastor C. Daniel LeLaCheur's legacy of offering hope and healing to people of all ages who have been robbed of the blessings God has ordained to give to them and their families. Not only have I experienced firsthand the power of the biblical message of generational blessing as Dan ministers it to Christian leaders, students and congregations, I can also give personal testimony of the life-changing impact this message has on a family: my wife and I spoke and prayed a biblical blessing over each of our teenage daughters in public ceremonies under Dan's guidance, and we will always be grateful for those deeply meaningful spiritual events. The material in this book can truly change lives and heal families. Make it a part of your future today!

Dr. David Cole
President, Eugene Bible College
Eugene, Oregon

Since doing the Blessing ceremony as described in your book, you can't imagine how much it has meant to us and how our family relationship has improved in only one week's time.

Pastor Doug Trentham
Bethany Open Bible Church
Tacoma, Washington

Dear Dan,

Thank you—Thank you—Thank you, for all you did for us. We will never be the same.

The Cottage Grove Church

The sixth grade Blessing was a time of affirming our girls, Kelsey and Keri, and giving them something to remember of the occasion. Gwyn and I had an opportunity to visit the Holy Lands and we purchased rings in Bethlehem for each of their sixth grade Blessings. Each one was different and special. It was a symbol of commitment from us as their parents, that we valued, supported and loved them, and a symbol of encouragement to our children to remain pure and true to their values.

Scot and Gwyn Burden
Spokane, Washington

A HOME OF PAIN
or
A HOME OF POWER

THE LEGACY LIVES ON

DAN LELACHEUR

Cover design by Alpha Advertising
Text layout and design by Pine Hill Graphics

Packaged by Pine Hill Graphics

The Legacy Lives On: A Home of Pain or a Home of Power
Copyright © 2004 by Family Survival Publishers
Eugene, Oregon 97402

Library of Congress Cataloging-in-Publication Data
(Provided by Cassidy Cataloguing Services, Inc.)

LeLaCheur, Dan.

 The legacy lives on : a home of pain or a home of power / Dan LeLaCheur.
-- 1st ed. -- Eugene, Ore. : Dan LeLaCheur, 2004.

  p. ; cm.

  Includes bibliographical references.
  ISBN: 0-9727279-6-5

  1. Parent and child. 2. Family--Religious life. 3. Parenting--Religious
aspects--Christianity. 4. Child abuse. 5. Psychological child abuse.
6. Role models. I. Title.

BV4526.3 .L45 2004

248.4--dc22   0401

For information: Family Survival Publishers, P.O. Box 2114 Eugene, OR 97402
10 9 8 7 6 5 4 3 2 1

To all the families

Mothers and Fathers
Grandparents
Children—boys and girls
Older sons and daughters

To you who have discovered
The Blessing

The acceptance—The forgiveness
The release from the past

The confidence that God created you
You—You—REALLY YOU!

May the Joy—The Peace—The Power
be yours to pass on to
those who come behind

Thank you Mardell for your love and undying patience
through my search
for these eternal truths

Danell and Jeff, Lynne and Jonathan, son, Mark.
Ryan and Danielle, Brandon, Jordan, Nathan
You Are Our Gifts

Contents

Chapter I:

This chapter lays the foundation for the entire book by likening the impact parents have upon their children to graffiti—it is a permanent impression. Whether pretty or unsightly, helpful or harmful, its presence is obvious throughout their lives. The results of writing such graffiti upon someone's life are highlighted in this chapter.

Chapter II:

The Father Wound describes in detail, and with many anecdotal examples, the unfortunate ability to wound one's children, by many methods such as apathy, misguidance, busyness, and a transmittal of wounds from his/her own father. The Father Wound defines and shows how it repeats itself in following generations. This chapter stresses the importance of responsible, sage fatherhood, and addresses Father Wound healing; the popular view of fatherhood and manhood; and the treatment of the opposite sex and other relevant topics.

Chapter III:

> This chapter illustrates the negative aspects of three
> types of abuse: physical, spiritual, and sexual. Physical
> abuse leaves marks that can last for generations. Sexual
> abuse is illustrated by a prison inmate who has seen his
> life changed by Christ. He describes how he was sexu-
> ally abused, beginning at the age of seven, and eventu-
> ally became an abuser himself, never really knowing his
> own identity. The final section discusses spiritual abuse
> committed by people in leadership and by mothers and
> fathers. Many people suffer greatly from this abuse.

Chapter IV:

> This chapter explains how emotional wounds from
> one's past can affect one's present life. The answer for
> true emotional health and peace is forgiveness. Several
> scriptures are discussed, as are several examples of how
> forgiveness has changed lives.

Chapter V:

> Parents help develop identity in their children. The
> author challenges the reader to define his/her identity
> apart from material possessions or achievements. He
> discusses the importance of disciplining one's children
> and tempering it with abundant and obvious love. He
> discusses how parents can traumatize their children
> with ridicule or criticism. What parents put into the
> minds of their young children can affect them forever,
> promoting negative reactions. Included are contrasting
> examples between one whose life is embittered by
> wounds and another whose life is whole and complete
> by way of forgiveness.

Chapter VI:

> The second goal of the Blessing is discussed, as are the
> rewards of discovering one's own destiny in life. It
> explains the need for parents to cultivate that destiny;
> it reviews the two primary reasons why destiny can fail
> to be developed as well as six declarations that can aid
> in claiming destiny as one's own. A story about recov-
> ering from past mistakes, and finding victory and des-
> tiny is included, as is a list of questions to help one
> determine one's own destiny.

Chapter VII:

> This step of blessing explores the need for having a
> vision about one's present life and future. It discusses
> our attitudes that can obscure clear vision; the defini-
> tion of a vision; what vision can do for an individual;
> and how to develop a vision in a child; and the impor-
> tance of a mission statement.

Chapter VIII:

> The first half of this chapter is devoted to describing
> different rites of passage from around the world that
> include a blessing upon a designated recipient. It then
> discusses what happens when a child is blessed; how a
> blessing works in the life of a child; and the essential
> power of a blessing. The latter half delineates the nec-
> essary steps in preparing for a formal Blessing and the
> required elements of a Blessing ceremony. Sample cere-
> mony wording is included along with photos of an
> actual Blessing ceremony and plaques presented to the
> recipients.

Chapter IX:

Mardell, the author's wife, writes what mothers can
give to their children. She explains the unique position
of a mother who gives great gifts that a father cannot.
This chapter challenges fathers to present seven different gifts to their sons and daughters. Fathers must pick
up the challenge and understand who they are in both
their sons and daughters lives.

Review and Study Guide:

This puts the challenge of blessing and parenting on
the line. The chapter reviews each of the nine chapters,
and presents many discussion questions on each subject. It can be used as a guide for individual or group
studies.

Introduction

W hat has happened to the family? Is it broken? Has marriage gone out of style?

Can children grow up healthy without a father or a mother? Or two mothers and no father? I don't think there is a single right answer for these questions. After all, there *are* traditional families that exist today. However, many of these families have a chink in their armor.

The title of this book, *The Legacy Lives On*, suggests that every family is generating a legacy; it may be one of pain or power. Abuse or a wrong attitude can generate a legacy as much as love and concern. One is painful, while one is powerful.

I write about three kinds of abuse: physical, sexual, and spiritual. There is no question that any one of the three can bring tremendous pain, heartache, shame, resentment, and life-lasting turmoil.

My purpose is fourfold. This book will help you to know:

1. How to recognize pain as a wound from a specific situation.
2. How to find healing for the wound and lead a satisfying life of joy, peace, and power.
3. What are the components of a parental Blessing, and what part do these actions play in bringing about a legacy of power.

4. How to create an ongoing Blessing day-by-day, and event-by-event. In addition, how to develop a special rite of passage that releases a son or a daughter into manhood or womanhood without undiscovered doubts and fears of adulthood.

This Blessing places an identifying monument in a person's life that they can always return to knowing it was here that their *identity* was verified, their *destiny* strengthened, and their *vision* opened to unbelievable vestiges of opportunity.

One of my grandsons, Jordan, had heard me speak on this subject several times.

When I began to write the book, one day he asked, "Papa, may I write the Introduction?"

"Sure," I replied, not knowing what was to come.

I think Jordan, now an adult, really understands the concept of the Blessing. My other grandsons have also added their views upon the subject:

Jordan, You're Up to Bat!

The other day at work, I was asked by a good friend, "What is one of your favorite memories?" One thing that you have to understand is that I work at a frozen yogurt store, and while pouring yogurt, I have plenty of time to think about the deeper things of life. So, I thought about it.

I told her that my favorite memory happened last year, when I was in high school, playing a baseball game at the local minor league ballpark and I hit a home run. I told her it was one of my favorite memories, because it was at a professional ballpark, it was one of the last home runs I hit in my baseball career, and it was just a perfect pitch that connected with a perfect swing.

What I failed to mention to my friend though, was that as soon as I hit that ball, both my dad and grandpa (a.k.a. "Papa" to all of us grandsons) jumped out of their seats whooping and hollering while trying to dial the numbers to call my mom and grandma (a.k.a. "Mimi").

You see, what made this moment one to remember in the history books of my life was the reaction of these two men. As I rounded third base, I looked up in the stands, and I could just see something in their eyes. I'm surprised their faces didn't hurt afterward, because their smiles were as big as half moons. My role models, the two men I look up to most, were proud of me. To a boy of 17, there was nothing greater to be given than love expressed like that. It was as if their love were open for the whole world to see, and all of it addressed toward me.

In every child's lifetime, there is a moment that can either condemn or affirm his future. Mine came two years earlier at my Blessing. The point of a Blessing is to affirm who the child is, and to release him to become the best man of God he can be. Wow. Afterward, I felt like I could do anything and everything.

Later, I had the hardest time deciding on where to go to college, though I knew my family would support me in any decision I made. Luckily, God called me into the ministry.

Blessing your child isn't just a one-time thing though. It should happen every day. A blessing occurs every time you make breakfast for them. It happens every time you play Monopoly with them, and every time you pray with them before they go to bed. It should be an active expression of love that is declared every day.

Oh, and one little bit of advice to you who have parents. Parents are just like us. They too need to hear the words "I love you" expressed toward them. Children can bless their parents, but just by being isn't always enough. Sometimes our parents forget that we love them. Remember, they are old; their memory isn't as good as ours. We need to remind them.

To Papa, I would like to say "thank you." Thank you for your love and support. I will become your stalwart oak tree. I will work hard, have fun, and have a focus on the now, and a vision of the future. Your and Mimi's legacy will always live on through your grandsons.

Ryan, What Does the Blessing Mean to You?

The significance of the Blessing in my life has grown as I have gotten older. As a youth pastor, I talk to many young people who have no idea who they are because their parents do not take the time to speak encouragement and blessing into their lives.

The blessing over my life, at 14 years old, was a specific time when my family showed their love and support for me in my entry into manhood and my continual growth in Christ. Those words of blessing from my family have carried over into my life and household as I try to bless my wife, Danielle, every day.

And Brandon?

I never really doubted that my family fully supported and encouraged me. I didn't have any reason to (with the exception of a few bizarre Christmas gifts that could have been misconstrued).

The Blessing permanently convinced me that I had an enviable and admirable cheering squad that wanted the absolute best for me. It is not just my dreams but *our* dreams. I am not just going places, I am being sent places. I am eternally grateful for what I have in my family and their blessing. Growing facial hair is great, having a driver's license has proven to be exciting, and college is fun, but having a group of people pulling for you is the best.

Nathan, Number Four Grandson, What Say You?

The night that my family gave me my Blessing was one of the most profound nights I have had. It meant so much to me that night and gave me a lot to think about in the days ahead. Being publicly blessed in front of my family, and by my family was a powerful gift.

It was a kind of intersection between my heritage, my future and me. It showed me that the family God had given me was behind me, and that they affirmed and supported me. That really stood out to me more than anything else we did that night. I know now that whatever happens, I have a family behind me. I intend to give a similar Blessing to my children as well.

❦ I ❦

Writing Graffiti on Their Hearts

On June 17, 1999 there was an anarchist conference in Eugene, Oregon, a city that is typically known for its beauty, diversity, mild climate, and rain. But to many people of Eugene, diversity means a rejection of traditional social, political, and spiritual standards.

On this day, almost 300 anarchists felt it necessary to demonstrate their ideals by smashing windows, stopping traffic, and in general, creating havoc throughout the city. When things quieted down, it became apparent that they had left an abundance of loud graffiti on nearly every place they touched.

A comparison has often been made between graffiti and a dog marking its territory by urinating on a certain spot to indicate its claim for that area. Both man and beast are non-verbally declaring, "This area is mine." Gangs have been marking their territory for years as they leave their particular symbols on surrounding walls and sidewalks. As parents, could it be possible that a type of graffiti can be written on our children?

It is interesting to note James 4:10-12, in *The Message* which states:

> *Don't bad mouth each other, friends. It's God's word, His message, His Royal Rule that takes a beating in that kind of talk. You're supposed to be honoring the Message, not writing graffiti all over it. God is in charge of deciding human destiny. Who do you think you are to meddle in the destiny of others?*

My purpose in this book is to show you the importance of certain biblical principals that teach you how to bless your sons and daughters. We will study how certain interactions between our children and us affect them, and then consider how we have the opportunity to bless our children in a powerful and biblical way. We will see the difference it makes in their lives, and what happens to them when we don't bless them.

We are not to write graffiti on their lives, because when we do, we meddle in the destiny of their lives. Paul said this in a different way: "Fathers, provoke not your children to anger, lest they be discouraged" (Colossians 3:21 KJV).

Yes, it is certainly a fact to consider that whatever your relationship with your parents may have been, it was the main source of your identity and destiny. Jesus shared an important part of His life when He said, "My father and I are one, if you know me, you know my Father."

Writing belittling words on your children's hearts, or leaving critical impressions on them, will very often undermine their confidence in themselves, leaving a significant wound in their spirit.

Three Results of Writing Graffiti

1. Shame

When a parent provokes a child to anger or bitterness, the result is a humiliating and dishonoring shame. Shame is one of the hardest emotional experiences to overcome. If shameful events or feelings continually happen in a child's life, they soon become imbedded in his or her psyche and can ultimately destroy. Colossians 3:21 states, "Parents, don't come down too hard on your children or you'll crush their spirits" (THE MESSAGE).

I remember the sad story that Leon, a friend of mine, shared with me when we were both 16 years old: His 19-year-old sister became pregnant. His parents were pastors in a church in town, and this news nearly devastated them. They were sure it would ruin their ministry and their testimony if any one ever found out the truth.

Leon told me that when his sister started to gain weight with the pregnancy, their parents sent her to live on a farm with an aunt. When she came back she brought the cutest little baby girl. But Annabelle could never let anyone know that she had had an illegitimate child. This little girl never experienced being in the church nursery, or in Sunday school, or any place where someone might find out to whom she belonged. Someone always had to make sure she was out of the house or upstairs in a bedroom if any church member happened to come by.

I often wondered what happened to both the little girl and her mother. It seemed to me, even as a teenage boy, that every time I saw her, she looked older, more serious, and hopeless. I think of this shame that was heaped upon Annabelle. Did she ever recover? Did she find love? Did her folks forgive her? Did she regain hope? Could the graffiti that was written on her baby's life ever be erased to set her free? If shame is written on the heart of a young life, it will continually eat away at the self-image and identity of that child. He or she will suffer greatly.

I have a friend who worked in one of the county offices in Oregon. She said that in recent years in its child guidance department, if a young person was delinquent, or had emotional problems, the department would most often ask the mother about the events and circumstances surrounding the child's conception and mother's pregnancy. It would be interesting to learn if the director of that department knew that one of God's eternal principles views conception as a dynamic part of the life that it creates. In God's eyes it is a holy matter, and when couples make it anything less, they open their home and the future of their children to significant problems. Every child should be taught the sacredness of conception, and that pregnancy should be taken very seriously and with much prayer. An act of intimacy that brings shame often leads to a life of inferiority and perplexity.

Each parent should paint his or her child's life like they were creating a great masterpiece. The colors for the masterpiece are honor, dignity, and respect. If the dark and dreary colors of shame are used in preparing any young person for adulthood, life will always be uncertain; there will be inexpressible fear; lack of self-worth; and most likely it will lead to the second consequence of writing graffiti on their hearts.

2. Abandonment

When abandonment comes about because of shame, both parents and child often surrender their intimate and loving relationship. Let's take Lisa, a young girl, who is deeply wounded and alienated from her mother and father. She became rebellious, cutting off all relations with her parents. Because of that broken relationship with her parents, she became lost. Who was she? Where was she going? Since she no longer had a solid relationship with her parents, she grew even more rebellious and began looking for an alternate source of comfort.

Lisa stepped out of the spiritual protection that God designed a father to have over his daughters and sons. She cut off the protection of her father and the nurture of her mother, the very ones to help her find her identity in life. Lisa went out in search of love. Soon she met a young man who said he loved her. They became sexually involved, and she was soon pregnant. Unfortunately, her foolish short-term choice of sexual satisfaction resulted in a serious long-term consequence because she was looking for love. Not wanting to have the baby, Lisa made a third foolish short-term choice by deciding to have an abortion. This action resulted in a long-term consequence of great guilt and shame over having taken a life.

Not too much later, another romantic relationship occurred, and she became pregnant again. Because she was still carrying the tormenting guilt and hurt from the previous abortion, Lisa chose to have her baby. She began to pressure the father of the baby to marry her, and eventually he consented. Each choice that Lisa made was an attempt to remove only the pressure of the consequence of the last shortsighted choice.

Lisa soon discovered that her husband was full of anger and very abusive. As a result, she chose to divorce her husband. Now she would carry the tremendous hurt and pain of the rejection from her father and mother, the abortion, the second unwanted pregnancy, the abuse of her husband, and divorce.

Once again she will set out on a quest for love and comfort, and all because of the broken relationship with her mother and father. Who knows when this repetitive process will end? She is lost, and only a miracle can give her a healthy identity and put her on the road to a positive destiny.[1]

When a relationship is injured, it takes far more than anger, ignoring it, or saying, "I'm sorry." Nearly always, the son or daughter is affected by the relationship, which has worsened beyond that which the parents could possibly understand. Sometimes, parents use excuses to avoid their responsibility saying, "He is just going through a phase," or "All kids act like that at this age." Be careful, your sons and daughters need a great relationship with their mom and dad.

Jerome, a 15-year-old boy, had a fragile relationship with his father. One day his dad said, "Jerome, let's go to the Red Sox game this Saturday." Jerome had anticipated this moment for a long time—he had lived for this day. He loved baseball, but he really just wanted to be with his father.

The Red Sox were badly beaten that day. Years later Jerome was looking at a journal he had kept when he was a teen. About that day, he had written, "I went to a Red Sox game with my dad, it was the greatest day of my life." He remembered that his dad had also kept a journal. At the entry for that date, his dad had written, "Took Jerome to a Red Sox game—they were skunked; a wasted day." Jerome was into his dad, while his dad was into baseball.[2]

I hurt as I write these words, knowing just how much every girl and boy longs to have a relationship with his or her dad. The terribly sad thing is that parents so often don't really know the role of their relationship with their son or daughter. They often abandon their children by thinking, "Oh, they will grow up." They *will* grow up, but with graffiti written all over their identity and destiny.

Inside children, the uncertainty of who they are becomes a major wound. Without the assurance of love and acceptance, self-doubt, fear, and misdirection begin to take over, and the wound gets deeper.

When identity is not affirmed, it actually becomes a curse instead of a blessing. When this happens it leads to a profound feeling of uncertainty and disorientation. The son or daughter begins to feel shame, and starts to self-blame. Guilt says, "I made a mistake," but shame says, "I am a mistake." If I *make* a mistake, there is hope for me; I can repent. But if I *am* a mistake, there is no hope. I can change what I do, but I can't change who I am.

Many people spend a lifetime trying to rid the shame by doing things they think will help, becoming human doings rather than human beings.

1 John 2:28 states, "And now little children, abide in Him, so that when He appears, we may have confidence and not shrink away from Him in shame at His coming." I previously thought this Scripture was concerned exclusively with the second coming of Jesus. Then I realized it is not limited to His second coming, because He is coming to me each day. Every day we have the choice of running to Him, or from Him.

Shame will most often compel us to run from Jesus—not to Him.

Here is the most serious part of shame: It leads to abandonment. If sons or daughters abandon their parent's presence, home, and philosophy, they will invariably abandon their parents' God as well. When shame leads to abandonment, very important relationships are wounded, and often lost forever. How can children be at peace with Jesus, when they are not at peace with their mom or dad? Remember that we are God's living witnesses to our children. The opposite of having a lost relationship is actively creating one of kinship, a sacred and wonderful family connection.

I have four terrific grandsons and I can now understand the proverb, "Children's children are the crown of old men" (Proverbs 17:6 KJV). Almost two years ago, when Jordan was 15 years old, he had a learner's permit to drive. My wife has a little red Acura that all the boys love to drive. One day Jordan asked, "Papa may I drive Mimi's car?" What a joy it was to take him to a local church parking lot and have him go through all the exercises of starting, backing, turning, and parking. I thought to myself, *I don't know if Jordan will remember this connection very long, but I am sure I will cherish these important and wonderful moments all the rest of my life.*

3. Hardness of Heart

In a regressive relationship, shame leads to abandonment, which leads to a hardness of heart. This hardness of heart occurs when the heart cannot be penetrated with the usual emotions of love and trust. When the progression of shame and abandonment leads to hardness of one's heart it becomes a form of personal idolatry.

I shall never forget the funeral of an individual of whom I had no prior knowledge. His family didn't have a church or pastor, so the funeral home asked if I would come over and do the service Friday afternoon. Wanting to make the eulogy as personal and beneficial for the family as possible, I had asked a few friends of the deceased to tell me about him. They all gave a fair account of his honesty, and characteristics of hard work, indicating that he was a good man and they would miss him a great deal. Thus, during my message I gave a glowing account of this man although I didn't know him personally.

Immediately following the committal, a man came up to me and identified himself as a son of the deceased. Quite forcefully, he let me know that he must have attended the wrong funeral.

"I thought I had come to my father's funeral, but this man you described was not my father," he said. "He was so selfish, and life was one big 'no' to him. He would embarrass me every chance he had, and that always seemed to be in front of my friends. You know, he never ever, *never ever*, told me that he loved me. Yet, he claimed he loved God!"

With tears in his eyes, he continued to describe his relationship with his father, and how he left home because he couldn't stand his father's God any more. Tears continued to flow as he stated that he only came to the funeral for his mother's sake.

I realized that I had missed the message of love and forgiveness that I should have given that day. This person needed to know that the Heavenly Father loved him more than he could possibly imagine. He also needed to know that most likely his dad didn't know how to relate his love to him. He was probably displaying the same lack of tangible love just like his own father had done to him.

There is definitely a God-created desire in the heart of every one of us that longs to hear the approval of a mom or dad saying, "Son, I love you so much," or "Honey, I am so proud of you." Some parents have never allowed their children to succeed in their sight. Instead, there have been doubtful, discouraging words expressed like, "You are not quite good enough," or "You could do better."

This was the case with Jan and her father. Her father grew up in the Midwest during the years of the Great Depression. He had always worked hard for everything he got. He had only completed the ninth grade, so he determined that his son and daughter would go to college. There was no question about it; they would attend college to prepare for some well-paying profession.

Jan realized the importance of education to her father, so she always took her studies very seriously. Much to her credit, she was a very good student. She started off with some difficult classes her sophomore year hoping that she might be able to relax and do some extracurricular things when she was further along. Nevertheless, she got an A in each of her classes except a science class in which she received a B. Jan felt very good when she presented her report card to her dad, expecting him to compliment and affirm her hard work.

"Jan, tell me why didn't you get all A's?" he asked. "What happened in this science class? You must be spending too much time doing things that don't count. You have got to work a lot harder. Let's see if you can get all A's next time."

He wasn't kidding. Jan was crushed; she had worked so hard. But she was determined to get A's all the way through. She did. But when she showed her report card to him with all A's his response was, "Well, it looks to me like you took a bunch of easy classes so you could just breeze through." She was blown away by this reaction.

Jan's dad could have really helped her, but he thought pushing and criticizing was the way to motivate her. He wrote graffiti on her heart and she could not recover. She was injured almost critically and all of her plans were suddenly disabled. Her grades turned from A's to B's, from B's to C's, and from C's to failures.

In her junior year she started drinking and running with a tough crowd and soon dropped out of school. Her father's dream became a nightmare. Eventually he told her he wanted nothing more to do with her. She moved out, got pregnant, and became a mere shadow of her former self.[3]

The progression of shame from abandonment to hard-heartedness became evident in her life. So many people repeat this process hundreds of times. We need to remember what James 3:10 states, applying it to what we say, and how we say it: "Out of the same mouth come praise and cursing. My brothers, this should not be."

Beware of Satan's Plans

Through the cursing of identity, Satan hopes to distance or replace your entire image of who God wants you to be. Satan wants to drive you out of your place of habitation, protection, and residence.

Blessing is meant to impart God's image of identity and destiny. When we write graffiti, or allow it to be written on the lives of our children, we are messing with their destiny and often cursing their identity.

Let's explore the ways to clean out any graffiti that might hinder the Family Blessing from being communicated. We will uncover the truths about:

- the Father Wound
- abuse
- the positive power of forgiveness
- the power of identity and destiny
- vision for the future
- an explanation of the family blessing
- the service of the family blessing
- what parents give their children, and
- what to do about it all

ৡ II ৡ

The Father Wound

M ost men will jump into activities at which they do well. And like the plague, they will avoid those in which they do poorly, or have had no experience in participating.

I was always happy to jump into basketball, football, softball, ping-pong, or racquetball. But, suggest surfing, scuba diving or hockey, and I would have other plans. Probably because I had no background in those things.

It's Like That with Fathering

There are a few exceptions, but the average man "fathers" much like his father before him. If a man doesn't reach out to his son or daughter, it is probably because his own father never showed him how.

Our society has endeavored to literally strip the God-given power of fatherhood from men. The world shouts,

"Who is a dad?" "Why is he so important?" "You can go to a sperm bank and get a seed; we don't need fathers anymore."

Most of the men who have been wounded deeply still will not be able to react to their sons or daughters in a way that indicates they know how important they really are to each child.

So he struggles in many areas, particularly relationships. He literally struggles after manhood, like he is climbing a snow-covered mountain. He sometimes feels as if an avalanche is about ready to fall and smother him.

If he has been injured by *his* father, the honest man discovers that on his own he is powerless to stand against the legacy of that pain. He remembers as a boy, decades before, when he was first overwhelmed by that same pain.

He subconsciously feels that he cannot save his father, or his own son, from this curse and destruction. He may even try to go back and talk with his father only to be rebuffed, sidestepped, or made fun of. He may seriously vow, "I will never hurt my child the way my dad hurt me."

What Is The Father Wound?

The Father Wound comes when a father wounds a son or daughter with a word or action that cuts like a dagger. It pierces the heart, and if reiterated often, turns and turns until the agony or shame becomes so severe that it is like an incredible infection inciting pain almost every day for the rest of that child's life. It never heals; it will affect everything that person ever tries to do. "A man's spirit will endure sickness, but a broken spirit who can bear?" (Proverb 18:14).

Sons and daughters can be bruised for life with a Father Wound. Daughters who are wounded go through life distrusting all men. Sons who are wounded go through life distrusting themselves, and have a difficult time relating to their sons.

Men who have this wound are suspicious of their own manhood. They are left with a serious hurt that causes various responses to surface throughout their life whenever a decision is to be made. That same man—who did everything he could to talk with his own father, only to be belittled or ignored—vows that he will never treat his own son like that. Unfortunately, he eventually does exactly what he says he would never do, and wounds his own son in much the same manner as he himself was wounded.

A man who believes that a father is unimportant will live that statement out when *he* becomes a father. All too frequently, he will follow in his father's footsteps, passing the wound that was imprinted on him to the next generation.

Fathers Who Get Off Track

George came into my office one day. He was the kind of person whose calls would always be taken, no matter *whom* he was calling. George was a major player, and his name struck a chord of admiration and envy among his colleagues.

He had not come by his profession, position, or fame by the connections of his father.

His father had been a farmer who immigrated to this country in the early 1900s, worked hard and was satisfied with life, even though he did not look like the picture of success in the eyes of the world.

George had heard my wife and I speak on a local talk radio program that we called *Family Survival*. He said, "I came because I have such a feeling of emptiness and I don't know why." I asked George what I felt was an insightful question into a man's priorities:

"What do you think is the key to your success?"

"Hard work," George responded. "There was never a job that didn't challenge me. I would literally days finding the needs and weaknesses of a company. In my early years, I was on call at any hour of every day or night. To me, being successful at my life's work was my highest goal."

Then I asked, "What do you regret most in your life?" When he started to answer, his voice cracked and I noticed tears in his eyes. I had clearly touched a sensitive nerve.

"I didn't spend enough time with my children. I am so sorry that I was never home, I was out spending all my waking hours becoming a success. I really thought that this would show my wife and my children how much I loved them. But when they were young, when they were growing up, I was never home."

Weeping, he went on to say, "Now I don't have a relationship with them. When I come home, I feel like a stranger."

Like hundreds of fathers before him, George realized that all those years of becoming a business success had cheated him from what he really wanted out of life: to be a husband and father.

George is just one in the great mass of men who has come to a place in life and realized he has missed what he thought he was working for. So many people, in building their home, get to the top, and find they have their ladder on the wrong wall.

The Curse Goes On

The following account has a dozen different variations, and I have heard it at least that many times told to me at men's meetings:

Fred had gone to live with his father after his mother had been killed in an automobile accident. Fred spent most of his days, when not in school, watching TV, and looking through his father's adult magazines.

Two weeks before his twenty-first birthday, his dad declared, "It's time you realized what it takes to become a man." They got into the old pickup truck and went to his father's "watering hole" where he spent about four hours every Friday night. Fred sat up to the bar with his dad and was served one drink after another. Fred said he did not remember going home that night, but he sure remembered the headache the next morning. Fred said, "I remember thinking to myself, 'Is this what makes me a man?'"

The night of his birthday, his dad once again said, "You need another lesson in what it takes to make you a man." They got into the old pickup and went down to the red-light district, where they both engaged prostitutes. This began a twenty-year cycle of drinking to get drunk, and having sex wherever it could be found.

Later when Fred asked his dad about those experiences his dad would say, "Well that's the way my dad brought me up. I just figured I needed to do the same for you."

Unless a change takes place, this type of behavior can go on for generations.

The Father Wound Repeats Itself

The Father Wound can repeat multiple times; that wound can hurt the next generation in much the same manner it hurt the previous generation of sons and daughters. A Father Wound can snowball down through the generations into a giant. It is a common enemy of fathers and sons with its crippling sense of alienation, shame, rejection, and untold pain. It literally mocks manhood and leaves even godly men shaking in their boots.

It is always a temptation to condemn your father for what he did or did not do, or for not giving you what you needed. Of course, this would only make things worse: During a question and comment time, a man in his 80s, rose slowly to state very clearly, "Whatever a man does not forgive his father for, he will do the same to his son." This man had lived long enough to see it repeated in the next generation.

"When the Israelites saw Goliath, they ran away in terror" (1 Samuel 17:24).

Remember it was not the adult males who conquered this deadly foe. In a strange and compelling way, it was a mere boy, who did not yet have manly pretenses and worldly expertise. He was a simple shepherd boy who still believed in God, and stood on his past experiences of faith and deliverance from other terrors.

When no adult man dared to face the giant, the lad took a stone from his slingshot and killed the enemy, the army of the Philistines ran in fear, and God's people were saved.

Only the Father God can deliver a man from generations of destruction into complete manhood. This is what He did through Jesus on the Cross, and will do for any man who invites Jesus into his Father Wound. Jesus came to restore our relationship with the Father, and to remind abandoned and unfathered men that they are beloved sons. Jesus went so far as to call His father, "Abba Father," which is interpreted as "Daddy."

It is true that the world has done everything in its power to devalue fatherhood and masculinity. From comics to movies and television, the father is most often portrayed as a buffoon. The media and advertising companies prey upon males who are cut off from their manhood, directing them to focus instead on style or money. Remember, a man who is taught that the father is not important, will act accordingly when he becomes a father himself. He will abandon his own children; if not physically, he will leave emotionally.

A Father's Importance

A wounded boy, in his psyche, tells himself that it is safer not to know how much his father means to him. To know how important he is to his own son or daughter, a man must remember and admit how important his own father was to him, or confess at least how important he *wanted* him to be.

This means that today's unfathered man must force the little boy within himself to face the Goliaths of the world. I'm not sure there is an easy formula for doing this. I still often wrestle with both boy and man, but I am convinced that it is vital to step from boyhood to manhood in a physical as well as spiritual and psychological way. Go back, as the little boy, or little girl, and begin to forgive your father or mother if they wounded you in any way.

There are many important steps between birth and manhood. Many of them are the physical development of growth and understanding. Along with these natural steps are the necessary steps of self-acceptance and the becoming of your true self.

As a baby, we need the nurturing of a mother. The mother is always important for that nurturing love. A child does not need a mothering daddy. He needs a man who is decisive, fun, and willing to show him how to take proper chances. Every son needs a hero, and the father may be the only hero in his son's life. That is natural and right because as the boy's hero, he can give great instruction that will never be forgotten.

A Powerful Story

Once upon a time, there was a king who knew that the next harvest would be cursed. Whoever would eat from it would go mad. So he ordered an enormous granary built, and stored there all that remained from the last crop of good grain.

He entrusted the key to his friend and this is what he told him:

> When my subjects and their king will have been struck with madness, you alone will have the right to enter the storehouse and eat uncontaminated food.

Thus you will escape the malediction. But in exchange, your mission will be to cover the earth, going from country to country, from town to town, from one street to the other, telling our tales, and you will shout with all your might: "Good people, do not forget! What is at stake is your life, your survival! Do not forget, do not forget!"

—Story by Holocaust survivor Elie Wiesel

Nowhere today is this call to remember more important than among men. Though we have been created male, with all the requisite hormones and body parts, we have eaten the "new grain" and forgotten what it is to be authentic men. We have forgotten the Father. For the new grain of modern secularization has brought a spiritual amnesia among us. We long for fathers to recount the story.[1]

The Big Mask

I often speak to various groups of people. A woman might ask a question such as, "What can a woman do to help a man become more sensitive?"

I think that many men who are super-macho are really guys who experienced a severe Father Wound, and are very frightened of their own identity. Much of what has passed for masculine strength has been used to mask inner wounds and insecurities.

Instead of confessing those hurts, men often only project them on women, or their children, wounding them just as they were wounded, keeping them insecure. So when I am asked by a woman, "What can I do to help my man become softer and more sensitive?" I understand. Yet, I am concerned because many men heard this in the 1970s and 80s, mistaking sensitivity for passiveness, which caused them to really lose their fire, and leadership in the home.

We need more than being sensitive to others. We need self-discipline. We also need courage to risk rejection when we speak the truth. We need willingness to accept the responsibilities of being real husbands and fathers

Fathers are every man's masculine root in this world. I think the most sincere critics of male behavior have failed to see that some men have clung to the macho image, remaining violent or alienated not because these traits define masculinity, but because they mask an embarrassing wound in men today that crosses all ethnic, political, social, and economic boundaries. That wound is caused by an epidemic alienation from the father.

This is a very serious problem for families today. This problem in the masculine soul is the gateway for destruction both in and through men today. The powers of this world, however, do not want to recognize it, because they have no power to heal it.

Healing of the Father Wound

One thing I've discovered in the years that I have traveled across this country talking to men's groups on this subject: If a man's heart has been wounded, then inside every business suit; every pair of faded overalls; and every sports shirt, lies a broken heart inside a boy longing for his daddy. The man may be hurt, he may be angry, but there is an innate longing from the son to hear from his father that he is accepted and validated as a man.

Every male child now, as always, longs to be one with his father. Remember, even Jesus said, "I and my father are one, if you know me, you know my father" (John 8:19). The basic plea of the male child says, "Dad, show me how to be a man. Give me fatherly protection, affirmation, encouragement, affection, provision, guidance, and strength." Every wounded man must therefore recognize his need, confess it, and accept God's help in dealing with it.

If left unattended, the Father Wound will become infected and ultimately destroy a man and even his children who follow him. The Father Wound is the key to understanding biblical faith. The closing verse of the Old Testament comes upon the threshold of the New Covenant and coming Messiah. God proclaims in Malachi 4:5-6:

> *See, I will send you the prophet Elijah before that great and dreadful day of the Lord comes. He will turn the hearts of the fathers to their children, and the hearts of the children to their fathers; or else I will come and strike the land with a curse.*

It does not say, "When I reveal my saving purposes among you, you will see mothers back together with their children again." In fact, mothers are already together with their children, because fathers are not present to take their proper responsibility.

Fathers Call Forth Masculinity in Sons and Femininity in Daughters

My wife tells me that when she took our young daughters to buy new clothes in the days of the miniskirts, she could always count on them asking; "What will Dad say about this dress," or, "Will he like it, is it too short?"

Not understanding the significance of this, I would chuckle and pass it off. Later I realized that my attention, my affection, and my approval confirmed their femininity.

Dads, be smarter than I was. I knew *something* was going on, but if I had really known, I could have shown more interest and done a better job. Daughters most often look to dad for this kind of confirmation and acceptance.

A man once asked me to pray for his two sons and daughter. He was concerned because they were alcoholics. I asked, "Were you ever an alcoholic?" He finally said that he was, but now he was an elder in his church. I said, "Is it true that your three children were at home when you were drinking?" He hesitated for a moment and then replied, "Yes, they were small children." I then asked him, "Have you ever gone to them and asked them to forgive you for your drinking?" He replied, "No, I never thought of it." Then I said, "I'm sure in their subconscious memories they have thought of it. You must realize because they never forgave you, they have retained your sin in their lives." The very thing they hated, they had become.

Forgiveness

We must understand the principle of forgiveness: It releases the victim. The only way to break the hold of Satan, and in this case the example of the most powerful man in these children's lives, is for that man to express his deepest sorrow for the example he set, and ask them to forgive him.

Suppose I am speaking at a men's seminar in a certain church. The pastor of that church comes to me and says, "Dan, could you loan me $100? I will pay you back before you leave town." He forgets, and I forget until I am on my way home. A year later, I am speaking at the church again; he hasn't remembered, but I have.

What do I think of when I see him? That he had promised, but did not *keep* his promise. He did not do that on purpose, right? Or maybe he is reckless and does these kinds of things....

"Oh, Dan," I say to myself. "Just forget it, you have forgotten things too." But now I can't forget. I want to, but it just keeps nagging me. Here he is happy as a lark, but I am bearing his broken promise. What do I do? Well, I either must go and remind him, and get him to pay me back, or really forgive him. I can't be released from the burden until I release *him*.

We as children must forgive our dads, or we will reap their sins. Like a Richter scale that indicates the severity of an earthquake, it doesn't measure incrementally, but exponentially. When we don't forgive, we retain their sin in our life, and the problem keeps growing. We embody the characteristics we hated in them.

Hiding from Manhood

This is something of which most of our world has been unaware. Too often men hide from their fathers, and thus hide from true manhood. I became aware of how far this Father Wound goes when a good friend of mine shared with me one evening after I had spoken on the subject. He told me that he had always resented his dad; in fact, he had been downright angry with him most of his life. Expecting to hear some sordid story of abuse, I asked Bob, "What did your father do to bring about all these feelings that you have carried for so many years?" He said, "Dan, you may not believe this, but Dad died when I was nine years old and I have resented that all my life. But tonight I believe I really released my resentment and pain that he was not there for me growing up. I really forgave him and asked him in my prayer to forgive me for the way I have acted." Regardless of theology, the church so often has failed to offer men healing. Instead, it offers an anesthetic, or a Band-Aid.

Thus, most men turn to the things the world offers as painkillers. For example, in a job, they might think "If I can succeed here I'll prove my manhood; I'll show my dad I can succeed." Or in sex, "I'll prove my manhood and see how many women I can conquer." This may be followed by pornography, and then a total lustful lifestyle, all to prove manhood. They may look for painkillers in toys like cars, boats, and lots of playthings, or through sports, participating in every possible activity to prove they are virile and manly. Or with drugs or alcohol, which can have temporary tranquilizing effects.

How Do Men Treat The Opposite Sex?

Some men in certain liberal churches are so afraid of oppressing women, and being called male chauvinists, that they declare themselves free from historical bigotry and embrace feminists who often are wounded by a Father Wound themselves.

So they may accept women who lead this alternate lifestyle, while leading a church. Or they may have even thrown out all biblical morality and call the deity Mother God. They run to hide from the Father Wound behind women, as they did as boys when hiding behind mother to avoid a fearsome father.

Males in certain conservative churches take a different stance. They are often so afraid of being oppressed by females that they make the Father God too masculine. They depreciate women in the church hardly leaving room for them to minister and use their gifts of teaching and preaching, or gifts that include the softer characteristics of mercy, compassion, and grace that are necessary to show the complete person of Christ and His salvation. So the conservative man says, "I'm not like a woman," and then he hides his pain by proclaiming a Father God modeled after his own exclusively male image. The liberal speaks inclusive language and the conservative speaks scriptural language.

Meanwhile, the crippling Father Wound cries out from a generation of men and women, only to be muffled by shouts designed to avoid meeting the true Father God. Deep in our souls a little boy or girl pleads, "Daddy, Daddy, love me. Daddy, tell me who I am."[2]

Nobody But Jesus

What does a boy gain from having a father present that men today must remember? Is it playing baseball or learning to ride a bike that his mother very well can do? Gordon Dalbey, in his book, *Sons of the Father*, gives a most intriguing answer. He tells of a thirty-year-old man whose father had severely rejected him:

"Sure, my dad hurt me terribly at times," he said, "But I remember once when my brother and I were about six and four, sitting on the bed with Dad with one of us under each of his arms as he told us a bedtime story. I don't remember what the story was, but I'll never forget feeling there was something about him that I'd never felt about Mom. Something hard to describe, but definitely masculine, like a kind of brown ooze coming out of him and going into us little boys."

Fascinated, I thought and wondered where I had also experienced this brown ooze. Then I remembered: I had a job shocking wheat for a farmer near Howard, South Dakota in the summer between my freshman and sophomore years. The summer sun was very hot, and I was wishing I had some fresh lemonade. I looked up and my dad was walking across the field with a half-gallon of lemonade and a sack full of cookies. He greeted me with the familiar, "Hello son, how ya doing?" Then he said, "Let's sit in the shade over there and cool off." We sat down, Dad poured the lemonade, then he put his hand on my leg and said, "Boy, does this remind me of when I was a boy on the ranch in Nebraska."

For the next few minutes I listened to my dad reminisce about his boyhood. It was then that I realized, with his big hand on my leg, and his voice giving out the manly vibrations of father-son identity: As much as I loved my mother, there was something different about my father. I think about the man who had the power to name me and define my man-hood, and something passed from him to me that is almost indefinable, but has always stayed with me. Robert Bly who wrote the book *Iron John* stated,

> When a father and son do spend long hours together we could say that a substance almost like food passes from the older body to the younger.... The son's body, not his mind, receives, and the father gives this food at a level far below consciousness. The son does not receive a hands-on healing, but a body-on heal-ing. The cells receive some knowledge of what an adult masculine body is. The younger body learns at what frequency the masculine body vibrates. It begins to grasp the song that an adult male's cells sing.[3]

Questions That Must Be Answered

1. Can Christians have this Father Wound?

Yes, and they can pass it on to the next generation. So many evangelists, church leaders, or traveling musicians have regretted the time they missed with their spouse or children. I'm sorry to say that dozens of them lost one or both in the contest between their ministry and family responsibilities.

I have asked the question scores of times in services all across this country. "Is there anyone here today who still wakes up in the night hearing a mother berating you because you are overweight or ugly, saying you will never amount to anything? Is there anyone here who still feels the shame of a father's word, or the anxiety of a relationship that you never had with him?" I have never asked these questions without one or many Christians saying, "Yes, I have a wound that goes back to my childhood." Sadly, this wound affects Christian families as well as non-Christian families.

2. Does your child know?

Does she really know that you love her? How do you tell her? Do you keep your promises to your son? Are you willing to do something he or she wants to do, even though it is boring to you? How do you react when your child says, "I hate you"? Can you get your son or daughter to be open with you about their problems?

Pastor friends Doug and Wilda Trentham shared this story about their son Chad: Wilda had volunteered to chaperone at a school function. She was not very pleased about the "dirty dancing" that went on, and vowed that she would never volunteer at another school function.

A couple of years later, their son, who was now student body vice president, asked her if she would come and chaperone at a school party. She went, and this time she thoroughly enjoyed the evening. Chad had gotten a Christian disc jockey to come, and had enough influence that there was no dirty dancing or even close dancing.

The truth is if we keep talking, praying, and influencing our children, they in turn will influence their world.

3. Do I really communicate?

A child's first and most basic way of dealing with his or her world is through emotions. A child is born with an amazing ability to perceive emotionally, and to be sensitive to the feelings of others.

Watch a child nestle into the bosom of a mother who dearly loves her, wants her, and is at peace with the world. Contrast that to a newborn who is handed to a mother filled with anger, resentment, and frustration.

Children remain extremely sensitive to emotions during the first five years of their lives. What does that mean to us as Christian parents? It means our primary way of communicating our spiritual life to our children is through emotional means: hugging, touching, kissing, singing, laughing, and talking.

The most attractive emotion to children is the one that attracts adults: love. Children don't just respond to love, they blossom under it. It modifies their behavior and character in a way that is far more potent than giving them information or a lush beautiful physical environment. In addition, what we tell our children about God and His love is even more important than what we *show* them.

4. How do we show them God's love?

Eye contact: They soon learn you are serious about your relationship with God.

It is important to look right into their eyes as you talk about that relationship and all the values that you hold dear.

Meaningful touch: It is amazing how some parents only touch their children when they dress them, or help them in and out of a car, lift them up to get a drink, or discipline them. They need many hugs from loving parents.

5. Do you listen to them?

One of the foremost complaints teens have about their parents is that they do not listen to them, and that they cannot talk to their parents. They want to, but they feel parents won't talk to them.

Make time for conversation. This takes practice; it is sometimes very difficult, but start with the obvious: "How was school today?" "Did you have a good lunch?"

If you do not talk to them while they are growing up, don't expect to start talking when they are teens. Flowing communication will allow you to talk about sex, drugs, peer pressure, and their relationship with the Lord.

❦ III ❦

Abuse that Goes
On and On

In no way am I an expert on abuse. Nevertheless, I know it happens. I know it destroys the future of many individuals. I also know it most often passes on to the next generation, continuing to curse the families it touches unless it is dealt with and family members are healed.

This chapter is divided into three sections: physical abuse, sexual abuse, and spiritual abuse. I will discuss physical and sexual abuse in an informative manner. We need to understand the terrible threat to individuals these abuses possess.

In the third section, I will examine spiritual abuse in a more comprehensive way as the topic has not yet been dissected by secular professionals, who most often classify it only as emotional or psychological abuse. I want to show you the spiritual dimensions.

Physical Abuse

"You little brat! Get up or so help me God, I am going to kill you!" The words just screamed through the room. Janny tried to hide so her father wouldn't see her, but she could see him standing over her brother Billy who was two years older than she. Billy was doubled up in front of the big chair in the living room. Janny held her doll as tight as she could and felt like it was her only friend. She saw her father grab Billy by the hair and jerk him to his feet. "You stupid little idiot. You were born stupid and you'll die stupid," he shouted, shaking Billy by the hair. Janny put her hands over her ears so she wouldn't hear the sound of her father slapping Billy's face.

Punching, slapping, hitting, pushing, biting, burning, and various other painful actions intentionally inflicted upon another individual are forms of physical abuse. They are usually done to those by someone close to them and responsible for their care and well-being.[1]

Often we have viewed the headlines: "Mother Accused of Drowning Three Children," or "Battered Wife Charged in Hiring Man to Shoot Abusive Husband."

Abuse occurs in all kinds of families—rich, poor, black, and white. The abuser can be your neighbor, friend, or a relative. Most of those who are abused try to hide the bruises, scars and pain. Most of them don't know where to get help.

I won't be explaining how to reach out for help, or how to recover from such terrible ordeals caused by physical abuse. My focus will be to enlighten families about the wounds from abuse, the pain that follows closely behind, and how the next generation often participates in this behavior thus perpetuating the "disease" of physical abuse.

For generations there have been some major misconceptions about abuse, such as the concept of, "What goes on in a family's home is no one else's business," or "Children are like property that need severe discipline." These concepts could not be further from the truth.

Many parents do not realize that such abuse can affect a child for the rest of their life, creating a hurting child who can become an adult monster.

Verbal Abuse

Very often, along with the physical abuse comes verbal abuse, a deep emotional abuse. When a child is being hit, or attacked physically, while hearing how ugly he is, or how fat he is, that child will always see himself as described when being wounded. The pain will be absorbed into how he perceives his looks, and how he feels.

If this is happening to you, in any way, please get help.

- Talk to your pastor.
- Tell the school nurse.
- Listen to your children if they indicate something like this is happening.
- Verbal abuse is more likely to maim the spirit and ego than the body.

Sexual Abuse

Mickeal in his book, *A Broken Promise*, relates an awful case of sexual abuse:

At the age of seven, I became the object of sexual incest and severe molestation by multiple child-sex offenders and two adult offenders. It was my next brother who was about nine years old, who initially molested me. Then three male cousins (of similar age with the oldest being about 12) sexually abused me over many years. Then six other kids (male and female)—all under the age of 12, as well as two adults took sexual advantage of me.

All of this was against my will, even at this young age. I felt as though I had a sign around my neck saying, "I am a sex toy, play with me." I felt very powerless, used and controlled when I could not stop their actions toward me. I really got confused. This stuff felt so good. But I knew it was wrong. Somewhere around the age of eight, I did the "right thing," and told. I was not believed and was given a whipping for lying. Then I was beat up for telling and was laughingly molested even while my nose was bleeding. I was told, "Now go tell again!"

I learned quickly that day, you don't tell because others won't believe you and you will get beat up. Most of the abuse others did to me was not painful but pleasurable. What they did to me, I soon learned to do to them. The abuse by my cousins, who lived on a farm, was very perverse.

Probably my greatest surprise and one of the great reasons for my demise as a real person into this lifestyle was that many adults knew what I was involved in, but they just turned their heads and walked away.[2]

Alice Husky, an incest survivor and author of *Stolen Childhood*, states in her book, "For a child to know that adults know of the abusive situation, but are doing nothing about it, is more traumatic to the child than the abuse itself."

Children just cannot comprehend the long-term effects on themselves or others, or how all of these experiences shape their adult lives.

Parents, please listen: Don't ignore the signs or actions of this kind of activity or abuse. Find help. God will forgive, heal, and cleanse. Fathers and mothers, as the spiritual, moral, and physical leaders in your home, you must take the lead and keep your children from this kind of harm. A child may not inherit his parent's talents. But he or she will absorb your values and behavior.

Spiritual Abuse

Jerry was around 35 years old at the time. I met him at a men's retreat in the Midwest. He told me that his best friend Bill had invited him to come to the retreat, but he had not wanted to come. When I asked why, he said, "You don't really want to know."

"Are you sure of that?" I asked.

"Well, I haven't spoken to a preacher in fifteen years."

"Can you tell me why?" I asked.

"I suppose…" but he only got that far when he started to fidget, looking for the door.

I realized Jerry was harboring some very strong feelings in his mind, so I reached out and touched his arm.

"Don't touch me," he jumped and shouted.

I apologized, but he only said emphatically, "*That's* why, *that's* why."

Undoubtedly, Jerry had some bad experience with a Christian touching him when he was a child.

"Jerry," I said. "I really want to help you, but only if you want me to." Jerry sat down in a desperate act of submission and started to cry.

"My dad was a preacher," he said as he unfolded one of the most brutal stories of spiritual abuse that I had ever heard.

Jerry had contracted a case of poison ivy and had broken out in a terrible rash. He was just miserable. He was isolated from the entire family so that no one would be exposed to it, especially his dad, the preacher.

He let Jerry know that he had to preach to his flock tomorrow. What would happen if he got this rash from him?

His father couldn't stand to have anyone think that he was less than perfect. It would be a disgrace to be weak, or sick, or particularly covered in an itchy rash.

Thus, isolated and miserable, the little boy sacrificed for his father, this man of God, whom he needed so desperately, but of whom, Jerry thought, God must have needed more.

Jerry shared another incident that must have been the final straw:

He had been playing with a couple of the church boys. Things got a little out of control and it eventually became embarrassing to his parents.

"Dad just walked in and grabbed my left hand and pulled me right out of there," Jerry related.

"In fact, he was smiling, but under his breath, he was yelling at me. As he dragged me outside, he took my hand and twisted it so hard that something popped. Excruciating pain just enveloped my whole body. I cried out so he jerked on my arm again. Later in the day when my folks realized there was something seriously wrong with my arm, they decided to take me to the emergency room.

"But they waited until it got dark so no one would see us. When we got there, my dad said, 'Wait here. I will be right back.' He went in and scouted out the emergency room to make sure no one they knew was there. Finally they took me in. My arm was badly sprained. However, my dad never apologized. It was my fault because I had acted as no minister's son should ever act. What would people think?"[3]

I now understood why Jerry never went to church. I understood why he had reacted so strongly when I touched him.

What Is Spiritual Abuse?

Spiritual abuse usually comes from authority figures who hold you responsible for their ideals of working out your salvation—or theirs. Religious leaders often use their position to control other people. They contend that a person must live up to their idea or revelation of spiritual standards. This leads them to do or not do certain things to prove their spirituality.

I remember as a boy experiencing services of divine healing by the laying on of hands. I noticed that the tendency of many people was to feel unworthy or guilty if they were not healed immediately. I even remember an evangelist saying, "Well, there must be sin in your life."

I have witnessed many wonderful healings, miracles, and answered prayers. It is part of my spiritual walk with the Son of God. But, when I saw spiritual leaders heaping a burden of guilt upon the candidate for healing, I realized three things: 1) They were absolving themselves from any failure in the person being healed; 2) They were placing this person in an almost impossible situation by labeling the person with a lack of faith or degree of sin; and 3) I knew that Jesus could, and does, heal but not necessarily in our time frame.

How Does Spiritual Abuse Arise?

Spiritual abuse comes when guilt or shame rather than grace is the leading factor in the relationship process. A recipient of this abuse develops a shame-based relationship. This person becomes powerless because of his or her experience in a relationship, preparing them for an abusive lifestyle.

We must not confuse guilt with shame. Guilt is a reaction to knowing that you have done something wrong, and you feel badly about it. Guilt is, and should be, a constructive signal telling you to repent and to correct your behavior. Shame-based relationships procure messages of shame: "You are so bad and weak that if you don't do it this way you will always fail."

Holiness is indeed an important factor in our relationship with Christ. But that holiness cannot be measured by do's and don'ts dictated through cultural mores.

Fifty years ago many young people were taught that wearing make-up, open-toed shoes, and certain kinds of jewelry was a sin. The sin of bowling, playing pool, reading the comics, and many other innocuous actions became the essence of multiplied sermons. Yes, it is possible that any one of these, or all of them could become a sinful act. That, I believe, has to do with motives of the heart, things that become more important than anything else, until they literally become idols of worship. But these things were often used as a means of control, rather than being an overt sin as described in the Bible.

The condemnation and judgment that so many suffered, detoured them from the grace of God and the love that should have been the foundation stone of their salvation. Many of these actions were placed right along with stealing, adultery, covetousness, murder, and the other commandments. This is where spiritual abuse leaves a sad and lengthy trail of embittered lives, poisoned—not from scriptural teaching—from a cultural misinterpretation of Scripture. They were condemned of contemporary "sins," not biblical standards.

I think of those troubled souls who came to my office with fear and trembling because they were abused or criticized due to something going wrong in their family.

For example, June had gone to a counselor and shared her problems about her children, who were misbehaving, and a very inattentive husband. Her counselor told her that her problems were spiritual because she was not praying enough.

She replied by saying, "I had hoped you could give me an answer, not blame me."

"Well, sister," he said. "It seems to me that you are in rebellion, I have heard God's voice, and if you don't take my advice, you will only have more trouble until you do."

With tears in her eyes, she related that she felt like a two-year-old, being put to bed without supper, and without any approval from her parents.

June's problem was real. It was not about her doing this or that. That was spiritual abuse by an authoritarian figure who needed to be "right," controlling people by saying certain things. June's counselor ignored her real problems and made her the problem. June questioned an authority figure who considered himself too spiritual to be questioned, and above error. Instead, her spiritual position before God was being questioned and judged.[4]

So many times, this type of encounter produces a most devastating dynamic.

Do We Do This To Our Children?

The scenario of an authority figure and a person in desperate need is similar to the one of the parent and a dependent child. Children are not given to parents to be treated as objects of ownership, but with the gentleness of the Holy Spirit and a Christ-like demeanor to lead them into truth with love and understanding.

Have you heard a parent say to a small child. "Billy, if you don't eat your carrots Jesus isn't going to love you." "Sally, don't cross your eyes, Jesus may just make them stick that way." Or even worse, "If you don't turn off that worldly music, God is going to send you to hell." There must be other ways to handle these types of situations. We must be able to think of some way to say, "I love you; I want you to do this," without placing a curse upon that person.

Whenever a person is left bearing a weight of shame, judgment, condemnation, and confusion about his or her own worth as a Christian, or person, it is likely that some kind of spiritual abuse has taken place.

A Look at the Scriptures

Galatians 5:1 states, "It is for freedom that Christ has set us free. Stand firm, then, and do not let yourselves be burdened again by a yoke of slavery."

Spiritual abuse is often very subtle and involves a strong church leader or a parent. In fact, it becomes a trap for both the person being abused and the one abusing. Both are trapped by a very unhealthy belief system. A child may be beaten into submission with spiritual coercion, or a church member might be receiving the same coercive pressure. A parent or church leader may be trapped into thinking that submission, however attained, is all that is needed. Not all strong leaders are abusers. But, when I hear them proclaim, "I am a man of God, touch not God's anointed," I have concerns.

Paul ran into this issue several times. 1 Corinthians 7:23 states, "You were bought at a price; do not become slaves of men." In 2 Corinthians 2:15 he states, "For we are to God the aroma of Christ among those who are being saved and those who are perishing. To the one we are the smell of death; to the other, the fragrance of life."

It is quite clear that Jesus took spiritual abuse very seriously. In Matthew 12:34 He stated, "You brood of vipers, how can you, being evil, speak what is good?" We see then how there have always been those who want to add something to God's grace. The Judaizers taught that salvation was all right, but they added circumcision as a requisite to salvation to make sure they had control over others' lives. These acts of spirituality distract from the act of grace that Jesus did for us all.

Through God's grace and the promises in His Word, instead of possessing a distorted self-identity that keeps you wallowing in shame, you can be released from guilt and shame. You no longer have to be a do-er; you are a human being created in God's image. Instead of being unable to ever trust someone again, you can associate with people through mutual trust.

Mark Twain once mused, "A cat that sits on a hot stove lid won't ever sit on a hot stove lid again. But it probably won't sit on a cold stove lid either." Those who have been spiritually abused will find it very difficult to ever trust a spiritual system again. We must make radical changes in our churches, and particularly in our homes. Being a Christian involves a direct trust relationship and unless we acquire that trust, we will soon drift from the real thing.

Our Children

Unless there is significant healing in children who are spiritually abused, they will most likely suffer from those experiences, and eventually become cynical Christians, or practicing agnostics.

When children are captivated by an idea or action, good or bad, it will affect them all their lives. Victims will remain victims, or they will rebel tenaciously, and go the opposite direction, turning not only from the actions of the abuser, but from the individual doing the abusing. David Johnson and Jeff VanVonderen in their excellent book, *The Subtle Power of Spiritual Abuse*, use this interesting illustration:

> Have you ever been to a circus and seen how a huge elephant can be restrained by a piece of rope tied to a tiny wooden stake in the ground? This is possible because the elephant was held captive like that as a baby. The rope and stake came to represent a force it

could not overcome. Now, even though it has the strength to easily free itself, it remains a hostage to a tiny stick.[5]

If we base our Christian home strictly on performance, there is a great possibility that spiritual abuse can find a foothold in our motivation. When we come to the end of life, it will be good to look back and see our legacy. If our legacy was attained by performance only, there will undoubtedly be several hurt, bruised, or permanently injured children along the way. If we give the impression that God will only be pleased by how many hours they work a day, or how large a salary they earn, they may never learn that He loves them unconditionally no matter how successful they may be.

Seven Steps to Climbing out of the Dungeon of Spiritual Abuse

1. Let go of your anger.

The person who angers you, controls you. Anger is a choice. Stop, walk away, and let it go. A good prayer reminder is: "Father forgive me my trespasses as I forgive those who trespass against me," (Matthew 6:12 NKJV). Use only positive and constructive words in your conversation. Plan ahead. When anger comes, what are you going to do with it? The anger is there, no doubt because of a real offense, but what you do with that anger is the key. Sometimes it is helpful to find a Christian counselor to assist you in this area. If anger isn't looked at closely, it can become a destructive underground force. Once explored with God and another believer, a person is usually enabled to let go.

2. Turn your criticism into praise.

When you are tempted to criticize someone else, think of how you can praise that person—even for a small thing.

People will follow your lead, and you'll notice that you will be criticized less, and praised more. 1 Peter 3:9-10 states, "Do not repay evil with evil or insult with insult, but with blessing, because to this you were called so that you may inherit a blessing. For whoever would love life and see good days must keep his tongue from evil and his lips from deceitful speech."

3. Learn to express love.

If you look for reasons to care for others, they can turn into the most important activities of your life. Such reasons to care will come more quickly if you begin to practice tolerance of others. The value of tolerance can be found in the following parable:

> Two Buddhist monks were hurrying late one afternoon to return to their monastery before nightfall. Unexpectedly, they came upon a beautiful young woman stranded at the edge of the same river they had to ford. The woman, they observed, was perplexed, pacing, and frantic. Like the monks, she was acutely aware that night was approaching.
>
> "The water is so high!" she exclaimed. "How can I possibly get across?"
>
> The taller monk promptly hoisted the young lady onto his back and strode across the swollen river, gently depositing her safely on the other side.
>
> "Thank you so much," she said. Now secure, she walked quickly to the road that would take her home.
>
> The monks started quietly along an adjoining path, but as soon as the young woman was out of sight, the shorter monk launched into an angry litany:
>
> "Have you forgotten your vows? How dare you touch a woman! What will people say? You have scandalized our order, carried our very religion into disrepute."

The taller monk, his head bowed, walked silently, listening without argument to the dreary, seemingly endless sermon. Finally, after an hour of monotonous abuse, the taller monk interrupted.

"Excuse me, brother," he said. But I dropped that woman by the river. Are you still carrying her?"[6]

Are you still carrying a heavy load? Begin to love. Work at it. It will begin to come easier. Love will come. 1 Corinthians 13:4-7 states,

> *Love is patient, love is kind. It does not envy, it does not boast, it is not proud. It is not rude, it is not self-seeking, it is not easily angered, it keeps no record of wrongs. Love does not delight in evil but rejoices with the truth. It always protects, always trusts, always hopes, always perseveres.*

4. Plan to be courageous.

Stop being afraid. Learn to take a risk. A risk is like an ever-widening span across an opening drawbridge. You don't walk or step, you leap across a risk.

Risks inspire fear because of the unknown. However, that can be so rewarding. You can change the negative in your life by taking a leap of faith, even if there is fear in the leap. Have you heard the old story of the little eagle that would not take a good look at itself?

Quite by accident, a farmer found an eagle's egg on a hill. He carried it to the chicken coop near his barn and plopped it alongside some eggs in the nest of a hen. Later, the eagle hatched among a brood of chicks.

As the eagle grew, it did what chicks do, since it was convinced that it was a chicken: It clucked. It flapped its wings to fly a few feet in the air. Like a real chicken, it searched for no more exotic food than the seeds and insects it found by scratching the earth.

One day the eagle looked up into the sky and saw the most dazzling creature it had ever seen.

"What is that?" it asked, startled by the sheer majesty of the form soaring gracefully in wide circles in and out of the high clouds.

"That," a rooster said in a hushed, reverent tone, "is an eagle, the greatest of all birds."

"Wow, I'd like to do that!"

"Forget it," the rooster advised. "We're different."

So the little eagle forgot. When it died a year later, it died believing it was a chicken.

Isaiah 40:31 states that, "Those who hope in the Lord will renew their strength. They will soar on wings like eagles; they will run and not grow weary, they will walk and not faint."[7]

5. Change you behavior and your attitude will change too.

There is another very old story about the widow whose only son died:

The widow went to the holy man of the village and appealed to him to give her a prayer, a potion, something to bring back her boy. He directed her to find and return to him a mustard seed from a home that has not known sorrow. The holy man promised that if she would bring it to him, he would use it to remove sorrow from her life.

The first home she went to was a lavish building occupied by a wealthy family. When the family responded to her knocking, she explained that she was looking for a mustard seed from a home that has not known sorrow.

"You've come to the wrong house," the family told her, recounting the series of tragedies that had befallen them.

The widow, made sensitive by her own loss, felt great sympathy for the family and decided to stay awhile and comfort them. When she left, she resumed her search for the magic mustard seed. She visited the high, the low, the middle, the rich, and the poor. Everywhere she went, she found homes with troubles. She ministered to all those she could help.

She was so busy helping others that in time she forgot her quest for the mustard seed, and she never realized that the miracle was taking place: Her activities drove the sorrow from her life.[8]

Change can be scary. There are so many questions: What if I stumble? What if I fail? Could I ever begin again? What if people think I'm a phony?

When you sincerely begin to do something, and God blesses your efforts, your whole mindset will change.

Luke 6:38 says, "Give, and it will be given to you. A good measure, pressed down, shaken together and running over, will be poured into your lap. For with the measure you use, it will be measured to you."

This verse is talking about life, it is talking about ministry, it is talking about who we are, and not your monetary contributions.

6. Forgive your spiritual abusers.

This can be very difficult, but it is very important. (Read chapter IV for more on this.) Begin to pray for real forgiveness, and pray sincerely for your abuser. You don't have to approve of their behavior, but when you release them through forgiveness, you are released from the chains that have bound you.

Matthew 6:14 states, "For if you forgive men when they sin against you, your heavenly Father will also forgive you. But if you do not forgive men their sins, your Father will not forgive your sins."

Remember, forgiveness for your sins is immediate. But more often, your forgiveness of someone who has wounded you is a process. That is the purpose of praying for the other person until your shame, hate, or bitterness is turned into genuine concern and love.

Julie Cole, a counselor from Eugene Bible College in Eugene, Oregon, has some very insightful thoughts on this subject.

> Often when I see abused people in counseling they are stuck in anger and unforgiveness. To insist they forgive at this point is often premature, and many times, they know they need to, but they are stuck. Their anger is actually pointing to the places where they need to stop and linger with someone who cares.
>
> Quite often, these places are where no one has ever expressed concern before. With time and care, forgiveness comes because the wound has been tended. I have heard of a few cases in which people have incredible, immediate inner healing and they can forgive, but most often, it is a process.

7. Pray for someone who is going through what you already experienced.

The strongest way to promote and maintain your healing is to minister to others, perhaps those who are suffering from the same pain that you have experienced. Here is a great Scripture, speaking of the spirit that was in Christ. Maybe you can apply it to yourself, and then to others. "A battered reed he will not break off, and a smoldering wick He will not put out" (Matthew 12:20). God is on your side. He will not throw you away even if you are broken.

Daddy, Take Smaller Steps

A story is told of a man who deeply loved his wife and son. He and his wife would put their son to bed, read bedtime stories, laugh, and talk to each other. Just before their son would fall asleep they would hug each other, give each other loving kisses and as the boy would close his eyes he would always say, "I'm going to be just like my daddy."

Then, knowing all was well at home, this man would walk uptown every night for a drink. Some time just before closing, he would stumble or crawl home. As a loving wife, she would wait for her husband, help him into the house and get him in bed.

This went on for years. On one special night it snowed, but it made no difference to the man. After the bedtime story, the laughing, hugging, and hearing his son say, "I'm going to be just like you, Dad," the man started through eight inches of snow to the bar.

Step after step, he made his way in the snow, closer and closer he came to the bar. Then just as he was about to turn the corner and enter the bar he heard a sound behind him. Turning around he saw his son, greatly struggling and trying his very best to follow his daddy's footsteps. The man looked at how hard his son was trying to reach each of his steps in the snow. He even saw his son fall as the steps were too far apart for his little legs, but his son did not stop. He would get up and stretch out his leg in his daddy's footsteps.

The man realized he had a choice to make: He looked at the lights coming from the bar, and then he looked at his son. So many thoughts went through his mind, comparing the fun of the bar life, and the fun he had with his son an hour ago. He just stood there with his back against the building, not knowing for sure what to do. Soon his son reached the corner and bumped into his dad. Then the boy looked up and said, "Daddy, you need to take smaller steps. It was hard for me to follow you." And as his father picked him up he heard, "Son, never again will you have trouble following my footsteps!" With that, he walked home carrying his son. They could be heard laughing, singing, and talking with many times the words, "I love you."

Never again was the man seen in the bar. Daily, the man, his wife, and their son, were seen walking, holding hands, laughing, riding bikes, and just being together.

❦ IV ❦

The Pain of Past Wounds,
The Power of Forgiveness

Unforgiveness is like you drinking poison and waiting for the other person to die.

—Wayne Cordeiro

Before we explore the power and benefits of forgiveness, let
us define the condition of unforgiveness. Unforgiveness is
the power of shame controlling a person's life. It is also the fear
that bonds a person's mind to a disastrous memory.
Unforgiveness is when one's identity has been captured and
held for ransom. Unforgiveness is the first step to idolatry.

Idolatry is making life's distractions so important that
they overshadow everything else. Paying special homage to
these distractions causes idolatry. This concept has already
been explained in a previous chapter, but it is important to
understand.

Unforgiveness is always idolatry because it gives another
thing (or person in this case) the ability to define a person,

keeping you fearfully enslaved to past events, emotions, and their effects. The sexually abused child, the adolescent son whose father deserts him, and the pornographic addict led into pornography by a family member, are among the many examples that can yield unforgiveness and idolatry.

Remember that forgiveness never submits to or states that an evil or sinful act is all right, it says the action is wrong. Willful and prayerful forgiveness are necessary to eliminate the threat of unforgiveness.

Read Hebrews 2:14-15 and 1 Corinthians 10:13-14 for more biblical insight on this subject.

Removing the Bonds of Past Wounds

The inclination to bond to our wounds, rather than move past them, traps us in a constant state of unworthiness. When a person who has experienced very traumatic events in life, such as the death of a father or mother, serious illness, accidents, physical abuse, and other such happenings, the individual can become bonded to that painful experience, replaying it, either in the mind and/or vocalizing the details, often for attention or pity.

These wounds of our past seem to give us an enormous amount of power over others. By constantly repeating the story of our wound and the consequent suffering, we create for ourselves more sympathy and pity. Our creative spirit can be so immersed in our memories of being wounded that it never functions in a healthy manner. We generate and perpetuate this feeling of being unworthy, in turn receiving the desired attention and pity.[1]

Testimonies of Unhealed Wounds

As a boy, growing up in several churches, and listening to certain testimonies of "saints," I knew something was amiss, but didn't quite understand the misdirection of testimony, faith, and sympathy. Certain people would always want to share their battle and then as they gained momentum over the months and years, find that they could generate a great deal of sympathy as they repeated the misdeeds that were done to them in years gone by.

Mrs. Pinkerton was one of those poor souls who accumulated sympathy each week as she reviewed almost verbatim the deeds and events of her husband who had deserted her and their three children; it really was heart wrenching. If only she had been directed to forgive and receive forgiveness, she could have started to live a happy life.

The Tale of Two Families

The following are not actual incidents of two families, but a compilation of people and events that emphasize truth and the point I am making:

The Broken family had attended the Church of Hope for four generations. In fact, the first generation had been charter members. They had accepted Christ there, done the yard work, volunteered for every necessary and unnecessary committee, loved the Church, and loved the Lord.

The second generation followed their example, but only because they figured that if Dad and Mom attended, it must be the right thing to do. They took up right where their folks were in their walk with God, faithful to the point of church being second nature to them. They raised their kids to be just like them; to respect church, with lots of emphasis on attendance.

The third generation knew the church inside and out. In fact, their parents and grandparents had a direct influence on many things around the church. But, times were changing. For example, the Jones family began coming to their church from a different church community. Bill Jones was now a board member, and he had pushed for a much younger pastor. He was set on bringing the church up-to-date.

Here are just a few of the new changes he pushed for:

1. Changing Sunday evening service time from 8 P.M. to 6 P.M.
2. Serving coffee and donuts in the Sunday school classrooms
3. Doing away with the church hymn books
4. Doing away with the church elders and forming a church council
5. Moving Sunday school to Wednesday evenings
6. Canceling Sunday evening service, replacing it with small home groups

With each of these changes, which came rather rapidly for the Broken family, a few of their friends started to drop out. Negative conversation flew in every direction. There were many misunderstandings. Most of their meals at home and other family times were filled with questions and then anger, which soon led to bitterness and more negative conversation.

After hanging on for about two years, the Broken family dropped out. They looked around at several churches. They even tried a couple home churches but that didn't meet their needs. The children have dropped out of church altogether, and nothing the parents have said will bring them back as healthy Christians. They will probably survive, but without healing, thy will have severe marks of bitterness and resentment in every area of their lives.

The next family, Unwounded and Blessed Family, were also in the Church of Hope that had gone through so many changes. They were also fourth generation members. When changes began—like them or not, agree with them or not—they decided that they as a family would never spend their precious time, meals, vacations, discussions, and at any time or place, be negative about other people at the church, or the changes occurring within the church. High on their priority list would be prayer for all the pastors, and the new church council.

Sometimes, the changes were very difficult; they did miss some of the old hymns that they had grown up singing, but that was never part of their family conversation. They often gathered around the piano and sang as Mom played "Blessed Assurance" and some of the other old favorites. The Unwounded and Blessed Family remained with the church.

The Church of Hope was led to plant a new church in one of the new suburbs. Mom and Dad began teaching classes, and were as excited as could be about the possibilities. Their two younger children were enjoying the youth group and the older daughter went off to college.

Remember, this compilation of people and stories is not of fairy tales. The point is that it is so easy to become hurt by someone else, or misunderstood. Often, that hurt becomes such a focal point in our lives that we bond to the wound until it is the guiding power of our life. It takes all our attention, time, energy, and spiritual power. It consumes us and all those around us.

Imagine that you have been physically wounded with a severe cut on your arm. An open wound can actually heal quite quickly. Sometimes it needs cleansing, and maybe an antibiotic, but if it remains open for a long time, or starts to close and is re-injured continually, it is very likely that it will become infected and ultimately destroy the whole body.

A wound must be closed and allowed to heal. When you lead with your injury, it can soon be the most important part of your life. Whether you intend for it or not, you will be held in idolatry to that wound.

Forgiveness is the ultimate antibiotic for personal, family, or spiritual wounds. Forgiving goes inward, then radiating

outward until it becomes the guiding light of love, and acceptance and hope for all that it touches.

No Forgiveness, No Healing

The exercise of being subject to unforgiveness can
become such a part of one's life that there is no room left to
advance spiritually in good health.

The effects of such negative actions are: allowing your
biography to become your biology, and your biology to
become your lack of spiritual fulfillment.

Wayne W. Dyer in his book *Manifest Your Destiny*, states:

> By hanging onto the traumas of your earlier life, you
> literally have an impact on the cells of your body,
> thoughts of anguish, self-pity, fear, hate, and they like
> all things take their toll on the body and the spirit.
> After awhile, the body is unable to heal, largely
> because of these thoughts. What this does is give the
> injured child inside you permission to control you
> for the rest of your life.

Dyer, then goes on to say, "The painful events of our lives
are like a raft used to cross the river. You must remember to
get off on the other side."[2]

Freedom From Bonding To Your Wounds

Freedom from bondage to wounds is through forgiveness. Forgiveness is the most powerful thing that one can do
physiologically and spiritually. It is, of course, one of the most
difficult and least attractive things to do, especially because to
some, forgiveness has the connotation of weakness or submission, as if the evil deed must be viewed as acceptable.

The symptoms for post-traumatic stress disorder is very
much like the results of an abuse that has never been forgiven.[3]

Positive Steps To Forgiveness

1. Recognize your hurt, pain, blame, fear, doubts, or addiction to the wound.
2. Read Scriptures. Here are a few good ones:

Matthew 5:23: *Therefore, if you are offering your gift at the altar and there remember that your brother has something against you, leave your gift there in front of the altar. First go and be reconciled to your brother: then come and offer your gift.*

Matthew 6:14-15: *For if you forgive men when they sin against you, your heavenly Father will also forgive you. But if you do not forgive men their sins, your Father will not forgive your sins.*

1 Peter 3:8-9: *Finally, all of you, live in harmony with one another: be sympathetic, love as brothers, be compassionate and humble. Do not repay evil with evil or insult with insult, but with blessing, because to this you were called so that you may inherit a blessing.*

1 Peter 2:9-10: *But you are a chosen people, a royal priesthood, a holy nation, a people belonging to God, that you may declare the praises of him who called you out of darkness into his wonderful light. Once you were not a people, but now you are the people of God; once you had not received mercy, but now you have received mercy.*

3. Ask God for forgiveness for allowing the hurts to become part of your spiritual outlook.
4. Forgive. This comes by making a real commitment to accepting God's help.

5. If possible, go to the person responsible for your pain. If that person is unavailable because of distance or death, write a letter of forgiveness, not blame. Remember you are not accepting what was done to you, nor are you blaming the other person, but genuinely forgiving that individual.

6. Put power into your actions. This will give you new and significant meaning in your life. Pray every day for love and grace toward the individual who caused your pain. Pray that God will begin to bless this person in every way, every day. You are turning the anger, hate, resentment, fear, and powerlessness, into a Christ-like action. "Forgive them Father, they know not what they do."

Forgiveness Is Not Just Spiritual

Becky Mollenkamp, in an article in *Better Homes and Gardens*, states that forgiveness research is new, but the findings so far are very compelling:

1. Anger-prone people are three times more likely to have heart attacks or bypass surgery than less-angry folks, according to a study that included 13,000 men and women. The study was published in *Circulation* magazine.

2. Men who are better at diffusing anger have half as many strokes as angrier men in a seven-year study of 2,110 middle-aged men conducted by University of Michigan researchers.

3. A University of Pittsburgh study of 680 women with chest pain found that those who harbor feelings of anger are four times more likely to have unhealthy cholesterol levels and a higher body mass index, which are linked to heart disease.

The article goes on to conclude that as hard as forgiveness may be, physically, it always pays off. I must add, there can be no exceptions to the power of real forgiveness, the benefits are always greater than the risks, and the results live on for generations.[4]

To Forgive Or Be Forgiven

Pastor Mark had just completed his sermon on forgiveness. He then said, "If any of you feel the need to reach out and ask someone to forgive you, or to forgive a person, now would be a good time to take that opportunity as you prepare to leave."

I was picking up my Bible, turning to walk out when I felt a hand on my shoulder and a younger man timidly say, "May I speak with you?"

"Sure," I replied, as we walked a few steps to be by ourselves.

"My name is Jeff Shelley. I think we met some time ago."

I acknowledged that I thought we had, and that I was happy to see him.

"You may not remember the baseball game," he continued. "It was at North High School. Your grandson was playing and I was the umpire behind the plate. You were somewhat at odds with a few of my balls and strikes calls, and were a little vocal about it."

That event began to get a little less fuzzy in my mind. This was my grandson he was talking about, who had one of the best batting averages in the city league. I was his "Papa." I didn't mean anything by my words, I was just too emotionally involved in the game.

"When the game was over," he continued, "I passed by you and you pointed at me and said, 'That was the worst umpiring I have ever seen, you were terrible.' I didn't know if you knew me, but I knew you as the minister and leader in my church. I was embarrassed and hurt. But I need to—and want to—forgive you."

"Oh, boy!" I thought. I am the guy who preaches about forgiveness, writes about it, and am now experiencing forgiveness from the other side. I could have crawled under the seat, and in fact, I looked for a place to hide. I really didn't know Jeff back then, a young man who was in a uniform and cap. Nevertheless, how could I have talked to or belittled *anyone*, know them or not?

What a jerk I had been. I realized that he was forgiving me for hurting him and I knew that I needed forgiveness from God for doing it. I not only forgave him for his feeling toward me but I begged him to forgive me for my one-sided opinion and thoughtlessness.

Today Jeff and I are good friends: not long ago I had the joy of attending his beautiful wedding. I have thanked God for His mercy, a great lesson learned, and that Jeff was mature and sincere enough to forgive me.

The Second Greatest Account of Forgiveness

When Joseph named his firstborn son, Manasseh, he said, "It is because God has made me forget all my troubles and all my father's household" (Genesis 41:50-51).

Troubles were not foreign to Joseph's life. I am sure Joseph had recurring nightmares of his brothers selling him to the caravan going down to Egypt. They had been jealous of their father's love and attention heaped upon Joseph.

No doubt, Joseph experienced what so many have found when they forgive the perpetuator of their misery and terrible memories. He said, "God made me forget."

I have talked with scores of people who have shared that memories allow, or force, them to relive events from their earlier days. I have talked to those who for 40, 50, or 60 years relived the deep hurt caused by words, or re-felt the abuse that took their self-esteem and shattered their lives.

The Memories of Joseph

Look at the behavior of Joseph's lineage:

- Abraham, his great-grandfather, lied twice about Sarah (his wife) being his sister.
- Isaac, his grandfather, lied to another king about Rebekah being his sister, just like his father Abraham did.
- Then Rebekah helped Jacob deceive his father into believing that he was Esau.
- Jacob's sons, who were so extremely jealous of Joseph then plotted to kill him and sold him into slavery, where he was eventually sold to Potiphar as a slave.
- Then when he rejected Potiphar's wife, she accused him of rape, and he was thrown into prison.

Family wounds can devastate a person's life. No doubt these scenes of Joseph's past had played over and over in his mind like a bad video. It isn't hard to imagine the feelings of injustice that could have welled up in Joseph's mind: "What a family, so unfair, so unloving! I never want to see any of them ever again."

Despite all of his trials and setbacks, Joseph eventually found himself second-in-command in Pharaoh's government. Many of us, if we received what Joseph did—out of God's blessing and favor—would have begun to assume that our success was because of our unique abilities, ultimately plotting how we could get even with our wicked and unfair family, thinking: "If they ever come down here to my territory, I will see that they spend the rest of their days in prison." When someone goes through what Joseph did, we often see vengeful plotting.

But it didn't happen that way with Joseph. Genesis 41:51-52 reveals Joseph's strength: "Joseph named his firstborn

Manasseh and said, 'It is because God has made me forget all my trouble and all my father's household.' The second son he named Ephraim and said, 'It is because God has made me fruitful in the land of my suffering.'"

Joseph displays forgiveness in a similar arena to that of Jesus: one of misunderstanding, dislike, persecution, temptation, and ridicule. Joseph also rose to the top because he overcame the idolatry of unforgiveness, depending entirely upon God for guidance and strength.

An Account of Life-Changing Forgiveness

Ada Wolf had been in the courtroom in 1965 when the two murderers of her son Dan had been convicted and sentenced to death by hanging.

Dan was a 19-year-old attendant at a service station. These men not only robbed him but also shot and killed him. Ada heard Antonio, who was about the age of her son, plead for his life, promising to serve humanity if they would spare him. Obviously, the jury hadn't believed him and sentenced him to die. Later the governor of the state of Washington had commuted the sentence to life imprisonment.

Thirty years later Ada heard that the murderer of her son was involved in prison ministry at the Monroe State Reformatory. She sent word to the chaplain that she would like to visit Antonio if it were possible. The unusual meeting was set and she waited for the day when they would meet.

Ada prayed as she waited; a phrase from the Lord's Prayer was whispered to her: "Forgive us our trespasses as we forgive those who trespass against us." It was like a light turning on, and she knew that she wanted to meet Antonio and that God would be with her to do it. On December 14, 1995 when she was scheduled to meet Antonio, Ada's son would have been 49 years old.

Ada was not prepared to see a tall, well-groomed man walk toward her after the guard unlocked the prisoner's entry door. Although he was 30 years older, he did not look like a man ravaged by the negative atmosphere of prison. As he seated himself across the table from her, he said timidly,

"I'm really nervous."

Involuntarily, she extended her hand across the table to him, which he enfolded firmly in both of his hands for a brief moment.

As silence in the room surrounded them, Ada began by saying that she had heard how he was serving humanity since his life had been spared, that he was a Christian, and that she was very interested to know about his spiritual journey.

Antonio relaxed and responded that he was truly sorry for what he had done and for all the pain he'd brought to her family.

"I deserved to die," Antonio said, "I really did. Saying that I'm sorry seems so inadequate." He paused in a silence of pain.

"Tony," Ada said, "I truly forgive you, but only because of what the heavenly Father has done in my life to enable me to do so."

She then revealed how the realization of forgiveness dawned on her 30 years ago that day in court:

"To my amazement, I discovered there was no hate, or sense of revenge in me, even knowing you had murdered my son and best friend."

She recalled how staggered she was at this realization; how incredulous it was to realize that God had done more in her life than she had ever been aware of—changing her from the cynical, fearful, sarcastic, negative person she had been so many years earlier.

She recalled how in that crowded courtroom, there came a sense of protection and assurance that she could trust her heavenly Father. Through these 30 years, that peace and assurance held her steady without any gnawing bitterness or burning rage.

Antonio then told her of his conversion, and the ministry that he had in prison. But Ada had a few more questions.

"That day you robbed him, had Dan asked you if he could pray?

Antonio nodded affirmatively.

"Did he pray out loud?"

Antonio nodded again, saying quietly and with reverence, "I will never forget Dan's prayer. He concluded it by asking God to forgive us for what we were about to do."

Both of them were weeping at that point, and as silence surrounded them, from the depth of Ada's spirit came the song:

> I worship You, Almighty God
> There is none like You.
> I worship You, O Prince of Peace;
> That is what I want to do.
> I give You praise.
> For You are my righteousness.
> I worship You, Almighty God;
> There is none like You.
> (Sandra Corbett—Integrity's Hosanna! Music)

—Excerpts from upcoming book, *Miracle of Forgiveness* by
Ada Wolf[5]

Ada discovered lasting, life-changing forgiveness; God answered Dan's prayer; and Antonio found Christ. Already hundreds are being touched by their lives, coming to a greater understanding and experience with real forgiveness in Christ.

God hears our most desperate prayers. Forgiveness is the key to unlocking the most difficult doors.

ৡ V ৡ

Legacy and Identity

Yes, of course I know who I am. My name is Jack Edwards. I am exactly six feet tall. I weigh exactly 196 and one-half pounds, and I have brown hair. I attend a university, and I want to do something that will help many people. Here is my home address, telephone number, blood type, and social security number.

The question is: Who is Jack Edwards? Not just Jack's idea of his physiological characteristics, or what identification he carries in his wallet, but what makes Jack, *Jack*?

We must consider more about our own identity. We know that our parents gave us our genetic code. Our address may say where we live, and the government gives us a number so they can keep track of us. Surely, we are more than the numbers and letters we own.

The Question To A Child

How many times have we heard Art Linkletter or Bill Cosby question a child,

"What are you going to be when you grow up?" which usually means, "What will be your occupation?" or, "How will you earn a living?" There is a lot of emphasis placed early in a child's life upon the occupational direction he or she will take. Sometimes the excessive importance put upon it yields an unrealistic concept of what a job or its by-products should do for oneself.

Does your job, house, achievements, education, or status define your identity? What if somewhere along the way you fail? What if your company goes bankrupt? Who would you be with no job, money, or a place to spend all day working?

Henry Ford, one of the best-known names in modern technology, wrote: "I don't think a man can ever leave his business. He ought to think of it by day and dream of it by night...." Thinking men know that work is the salvation of the race, morally, physically, and socially. Work does more than get us a living: it gets us a life.

President Calvin Coolidge wrote with a similar attitude, "The man who builds a factory builds a temple. The man who works there worships there."

I looked at men, whose whole life centered on their job, and wondered what their identity would be if they lost that job. A person is far more than their job.

Garbage In, Garbage Out

Let's look to the Scriptures. Colossians 3:20-21 states, "Children, obey your parents in everything, for this pleases the Lord. Fathers, do not embitter your children, or they will become discouraged."

The Message Bible admonishes this way, "Parents, don't come down too hard on your children or you'll crush their spirits."

There is always the need for a balanced relationship between parents and children, which includes discipline balanced with love; and freedom balanced with boundaries.

Distance

If the parent is too distant, or too easy-going—the child is likely to grow up undisciplined, facing life carelessly. At the very least the child wants boundaries, or he or she will feel insecure. This often becomes obvious as the child begins to intentionally (or subconsciously) do attention-getting actions in order to get direction.

Too Much Constraint

There is also danger in the overly conscientious parent who perpetually corrects or rebukes the son or daughter. We are reminded of the tragic question of a lady—who eventually came to have mental problems—"Why is it that I never seem to be able to do anything to please my mother?" John Newton mused, "I know my father loved me—but he did not want me to see it." Constant criticism is most often the product of misguided love.

The danger of all this is that a child becomes discouraged, then rebellious, and then loses faith. Like the Scripture states, "They will become discouraged if the parent comes down too hard on them."

Martin Luther's father was so stern that he said, "For all my life I found it hard to pray the words, 'Our father.'" The word "father" in his mind stood for nothing but severity. If only Luther could have felt that along with that severity was a father's love for his son. Parents—by relating to their son or daughter—influence their child's identity far more than they can possibly imagine.

Discipline and Forbearance with Love

Indeed parents give us gifts good and bad, and they affect just about everything that their children do in life. These attitudes, characteristics, values, and reactions are formed in the early years of our lives. They will affect most of our decisions, our relationships and our confidence in approaching all of life. Who we really are will determine how we handle each success and failure.

Tone of voice, words, and their intent, all have great influence on who we become. Think of the thousands of homes ravaged by abuse, anger, fear, rejection, and shame. To receive honor one must be honorable. Fathers, do not embitter your children lest they turn away from your teaching, your guidance, and your arms because of bitterness. Give your children the opportunity of a long life.

Who Are You?

Some people, particularly men, find ego fulfillment through what they do. When asked to define themselves, they invariably will give you their title or a name of what they do: "I am Doctor so and so," or "I am a reverend, nurse, judge, teacher, landscaper, or a housewife." These titles merely describe our job. They do not describe our identity.

"As A Man Thinketh in His Heart, So is He."

There is an account in Craig Hill's book *The Ancient Paths* about a man named Joe. Joe was a Christian and a successful businessman in his late 30s who had a tremendous problem with anger. One day after an embarrassing and un-Christian-like experience, he went to his pastor. They determined that when Joe was about 10 years old he had some friends over for the night. They popped popcorn, watched a couple scary movies, and went to bed about one o'clock. When Joe woke up he realized he had wet the bed, he was embarrassed and didn't want his mother to find the sheets, so he hid them in the closet.

When she came up, she found them, and told his father that Joe had wet the bed.

Upon Joe's entrance into the kitchen where his friends had already gathered, his father greeted him with the words, "Good morning, bed-wetter." Then he pulled Joe's pants down and spanked his bare bottom. "I could have killed my dad that day," Joe said. "He kept saying I was a bed-wetter, and I would never be more than a bed-wetter."

Joe then went on to say that every time in life that he was to make a major decision, he could still hear his dad say, "You will never be more than a bed-wetter."[1]

A person I met on a trip to Ohio told me this story: A boy's father thought it was so much fun to turn out all the lights and jump out and scare little Johnny as he walked down the hallway to bed. One night as he was walking down the hall, his dad let out a terrible banshee scream and threw a blanket over his head. Johnny passed out, and when he came to, his dad was laughing and said, "Johnny, you are such a big sissy."

"You know, I never was able to conquer that fear," Johnny said. "Even to this day I find it almost impossible to go into the dark. And that's not all. Every time I need to make a major decision, I'm afraid I will fail, or even pass out. I always hear my dad's voice telling me that I am such a sissy."

These are just two identifiable characteristics that can come out of such traumatic experiences. These events enforced negative aspects of their identity. Perhaps you can relate to such experiences.

Life-Directing Force

In the years between birth and six years of age most of one's brain cells are formed. From a study done at the University of Oregon, specialists know that it is what the parents put into the minds of their children in these first six years that essentially determines how much their child will be able to learn. If this is true with our minds, you can imagine how important are the impressions that go into that spirit of our sons and daughters through words, relationships, and actions.

Identity Is Not...

1. Identity is not your looks.

Hollywood has stressed beautiful looks and gorgeous bodies to the point that many young people actually believe that if they could look or be like a certain movie star, or model, they could conquer the world. But one's physical appearance is a far cry from one's true identity. 1 Samuel 16:7 states, "God looks on the heart, and not on the outward appearance."

2. Identity is not your intelligence.

Some people have very high IQs, and others take tests very well. This does not mean that their identity is incumbent upon their intelligence. Proverbs 6:12 states, "Do you see a man wise in his own eyes? There is more hope for a fool than for him." And 1 Corinthians 1:25 states, "For the foolishness of God is wiser than man's wisdom."

3. Identity is not your strength.

I've known many young men who want to be strong. There is certainly nothing wrong with pumping iron, or staying in shape, but one's identity is not derived by one's strength. There are some very good role models who are athletes, but not all professional athletes are good role models.

1 Corinthians 12:9 encourages us: "My grace is sufficient for you, for my power is made perfect in weakness."

4. Identity is not your earthly accomplishments.

Freddie was always rebellious. His parents had tried everything they could think of to get him to be an example to the kids in the youth group. It was the summer between his junior and senior years of high school. Freddie had landed a job at a sports equipment store. He had only worked there two weeks when his dad received a phone call from the store manager demanding he be there in 20 minutes. He soon learned that his son had stolen a $300 sports watch. The manager was threatening to call the police and have Freddie hauled off to jail. When the parents entered the office of the manager, the father really lost his cool, and started yelling at his son:

"Now look what you have done to us. Haven't we done enough for you? You can't imagine how you have hurt your mother and me."

What has gone wrong here? The father's response seemed normal. After all, they have spent thousands of dollars raising their son, sleepless nights, and endless hours of worry. Yes, years of hard work. They wanted to be good parents, and had really tried. What did they get in return? A kick in the teeth that really hurt—public disgrace.

I must ask, what had been this father's attitude toward this son over the years? What seemed to be his big concern? He had made a major investment in his son, and now the investment had turned bad. He had expected to get something in return for his sacrifice. His son was supposed to be like any good investment and be a credit to him. The father's hurt was so intense, that he couldn't even think of his son's pain, shame, anger, and fear. The father ignored all this because of the damage to his own identity.

5. Identity is not your humility.

This is true especially if it is a false humility that says, "I'm humble and proud of it." Some people develop a spiritual pride, and it is amazing how it changes their voice, and their viewpoint of others.

Colossians 2:18-19 states,

> *Do not let anyone who delights in false humility and the worship of angels disqualify you for the prize. Such a person goes into great detail about what he has seen, and his unspiritual mind puffs him up with idle notions. He has lost connection with the Head, from whom the whole body, supported and held together by its ligaments and sinews, grows as God causes it to grow.*

The real identity, the significant inner qualities of one's life, come from that early influence of parents and family. It comes from a positive, loving, spiritual input into young lives. Unfortunately, identity also comes from exactly the opposite kind of influence. Parents also have a negative effect upon their children if they abuse them in any way. Small children are like sponges that absorb both water and acid. Eventually, what they have been given will affect their idea of who they are, and this will manifest itself as time goes by. One's real identity comes through when decisions must be made, and temptations dealt with and conquered. Every choice is determined by one's identity.

Children and the Meaning of Life

There is no question of the parent's pain and disappointment in the previous situation, but the father viewed the incident as something that happened to him and his wife rather than to their son. Their value as people depended upon the success of their son. Sometimes child-identity parents are more concerned about the way the child maintains the family image than how they maintain the image of God. Sometimes pastors are guilty of this more than anyone else. They want their children to be perfect examples to others, or their ministry might be hurt.

The most destructive result of this invested identity is that it puts a heavy load upon children who are too small to carry it. Children soon learn that they are not as important as their performance.

More Than Psychological

The Scripture says, "Fathers, provoke not your children to anger, lest they be discouraged"(Colossians 3:21 KJV). "If the hearts of the fathers and the children aren't turned to one another, the Lord will send a curse upon the land" (Malachi 4:5 KJV).

When a child has been injured in some way by a parent, this injury becomes a factor in the child's identity. If you have been injured and have received mixed messages as to your identity, the answer can be found in Christ. "Behold what manner of love the Father hath bestowed upon us, that we should be called the sons of God" (1 John 3:1 KJV). He forgives thus you are forgiven. You are absolutely a new creation. This should be the ultimate characteristic of our identity. "Old things pass away and behold all things become new" (1 Corinthians 5:17).

God's Fingerprint

Many times peace will not come until the wounded person forgives the one who did the wounding. This action to forgive is really God's fingerprint upon our spirit. The Holy Spirit has been given to secure that identity. Ephesians 4:30 states, "Do not grieve the Holy Spirit of God, by whom ye are sealed for the day of redemption." The identity crisis is over because "I can do all things through Christ who strengthens me" (Philippians 4:13).

The child of God does not seek self-worth as an end in itself. He knows the search is hopeless. When our self-worth has been molded by God's agent, and fingerprinted by the Holy Spirit; then all the powerful consequences begin to take place in our lives. Remember that:

- The joy of the Lord is our strength
- The peace of the Lord is our contentment
- The presence of the Lord is our security
- The will of the Lord is our success

A friend of mine, John DeVriese wrote a book titled *Unexpected Joy*. In it he states, "You never find joy when you are looking for it, real joy always comes unexpectedly when you are doing the right things."[2]

Forgiveness Is Release

If, as a child or young adult, you had your identity badly injured, you can find healing. This kind of healing often requires that one release the cause or curse of that pain. Not only must we accept ourselves as a new person in Christ, we must release the person through whom came the injuring of our identity. The only permanent way to relinquish the pain is to forgive them. Jesus said in Matthew 6:14, "For if you forgive men when they sin against you, your heavenly Father will also forgive you. But if you do not forgive men their sins, your Father will not forgive your sins."

Invariably in a teaching session in which I have talked about forgiving someone who has wounded us in a serious manner I get this question: "Are you saying that when I forgive someone for something they did against me, what they did is now all right?" My answer is always: Absolutely not! When you forgive someone you are breaking the chains that have bound you. Usually it binds them to you through memory, disgust, fear, or even hate. Your decision of forgiveness, releases you from their power over you.

Reaction to Identity Crisis

1. Cutting a parent out of your life

Very often if a person has been crushed by a parent, his or her reaction may be something like this: "If he won't bless me, I don't need him. I don't even want his acceptance. It only brings me pain, so it won't matter."

The problem in attempting to cut the parent out of your life is that it actually binds you to that parent. Often you set into action internal and emotional forces that reproduce those same attitudes and actions in you, which you hated so much in that parent.

2. Striving after parental approval or blessing no matter what it takes

I have seen men become workaholics because they want to succeed in their parent's eyes, thinking: "If I can reach a certain status, make enough money, or even win enough people to Christ, then they will have to acknowledge me and bless me."

In striving excessively after the approval of a parent, you bind yourself to that parent and are never free to cleave to your spouse.

3. Attempting to do everything right all the time to enable your son or daughter to success

Success is a sure thing, until you factor in fate, luck, circumstances, health, heredity, birth order; a first encounter with evil; a first person to fall in love with who subsequently jilts you; missed opportunities; failed attempts; dishonesty of the person in charge of the pension; accidents. You get the idea.

In other words, there are many things in life that we cannot control or manipulate, but in spite of all these things we need to be convinced that God loves us and that He answers prayer, and even when we and our family go through the worst of times, He will give us courage, wisdom, and faith to come out on the other side—not just unscathed, but mentally and spiritually stronger.

I think of my many years in the ministry: the preaching, counseling, and begging of people to change; the praying for hurting, angry, bitter, desperate people, many who were mad at God, or mad at their mother or father. It wasn't until I realized that forgiveness, not just for our sins, but for those who have sinned against us, is perhaps the strongest force that we will ever have at our disposal.

The Last Chapter of Life

I have been by the bedside of dozens of dying people. Sometimes it is very ugly. Sometimes it is absolutely beautiful. I have not just watched people die, but *how* they die.

In Oregon where assisted suicide is legal, I have been compelled to think about the physical nature of death, as well as the spiritual nature. I will admit that death is not always easy. Some good people do suffer, but most of the time it is not the physical pain of dying that is unbearable. I believe that the dying person does not suffer as much as the loving people who are standing by.

We have heard assisted suicide called "death with dignity." But the loss of dignity is not the loss of life. The loss of dignity is often the bitter, demanding, loaded-down-with-regret experienced by the one dying, and by the family members who never received love and blessing from one another. The unresolved anger toward an identity that was wounded and now is too late to heal. Many who had countless opportunities to forgive, or to help a new generation be healthy will never have another chance.

When you understand their suffering, you understand why they want a doctor to be responsible for their last great uncertainty and administer that fatal dose of poison.

I have watched people die from virtually the same causes. One may die yelling and screaming all the way, whereas the other moves majestically into the throne room of eternity. What makes the difference?

Different Death Experiences

I visited old Bill in the hospital. We both knew he didn't have long to live. I read Scriptures and prayed, and gave Bill words of comfort as best I could. There was no doubt he had several unresolved things that were bothering him. Bill had always been very stoic, not too communicative even with his family. He asked me four times if I thought young Bill, his oldest son, was all right. I kept asking him, "Why, what about Bill makes you so concerned?" He would never say.

Four days later I learned—in a dramatic fashion—of the problem that ate at the heart of old Bill. The service was over, the casket had been opened and the friends and family had marched past paying their last respects. Young Bill held back until nearly every one was out of the chapel. He slowly walked up to his father who lay in the casket, and stood there for several moments. He began to cry.

All of a sudden he shouted, "Dad, you never told me. Not once, Dad, did you ever say you loved me." By now, young Bill was in the casket lying on top of his father sobbing.

What a difference it would have been for both father and son, if the father could have put away his fear and lifelong training, and just said, "Bill, I love you."

The Day Bert Died

I won't forget the day Bert Newton died. Bert was a member of our church in Des Moines, Iowa. He had taught a boys' Sunday school class for years. Dozens of boys had gone through his class, and I never met a man, who had been one of those boys, who didn't love and cherish his time with Bert. I don't know how good his teaching of the material was, but from listening to many men who had been there, I soon learned how much he cared for each of them. Bert's legacy rang loud and clear throughout the homes in that church and in the community.

I stood at the foot of his bed with his daughter, Gertrude. His body and mind had already started to die, and the doctor told us it would only be a short time before he was gone. While we stood there we visited about the memories that his daughter had of him. We prayed together, and then got caught up in the process of just waiting.

We could almost see as well as sense that Bert was soon going to leave us. But we weren't ready for what happened just before his spirit left his body. His eyes opened, although they held no recognition of his daughter or his pastor. It was as if a light suddenly came on and he could see. In fact the dullness of his eyes was gone and he looked right over our heads as if someone he knew had walked into the room. I thought he might speak, but he never did. He had a look of amazement and then peace as he saw what both Gertrude and I always believed was an angel.

He then relaxed and left us to be with his God. Oh, what a homegoing. I shall never forget the power of that moment.

An Apple Doesn't Fall Far from the Tree

Identity, this characteristic that is bestowed by fathers and mothers is both wonderful and frightening at the same time.

The frightening part is when parents don't really know who they are, they pass the same ignorance of identity on to their son or daughter. If they are an abuser, name caller, or involved in some kind of spiritism, they can pass these traits on as a wound or an overpowering force in that son or daughter's life.

God intended for fathers and mothers to be the major influence for righteousness in the lives of their children. This godly blessing is, without a doubt, the overriding sense of answering the "Who Am I?" question.

I have talked to many men in midlife, who indicate they are empty in so many ways. They have a longing that was not being fulfilled by their work or their wives. Upon getting to the bottom of their problem, I would realize that their emptiness was due to their lack of identity.

Identity is something that parents pass on to their children, particularly between fathers and sons. I remember one man, a truck driver, who said, "I just wish my dad would have told me when it was that I reached manhood, so I would have really known."

There is grace and love in a parent who can repeat often to his or her child: "You can do it," "You are special," "I believe in you," or, "Now that you are a man (or lady) God has a great plan for your life."

Ask, "Who Am I?"

Have you ever considered how you came to be born as *you*? Consider this, if there are two hundred million spermatozoa in a single ejaculation, there could be the potential for 200 million human beings. This represents only one sexual act.

Consider that your mother had 200 million chances to be exactly who *she* is, and that your father had another 200 million chances to be who *he* is.

We might say that the chances of you being born are 200 hundred million multiplied by 200 hundred million, multiplied by 200 million, multiplied by whatever chances that each of your ancestors met in the first place to eventually create you.

That is a billions to one chance! Who would ever place a bet with those kinds of odds?

Only God

Yes, you are unique; one of a kind. Your *heredity* produces your genetic code, which has much to do with the color of your eyes and whether you will have straight or curly hair.

Heredity determines how fast you can run, or how much information you can retain, and how tall or short you will be. Your *environment* provides the space for you to operate, and gives you the freedom to develop these gifts.

Heredity is the potential for what you can do. *Environment* is your opportunity.

We are presented our *heredity* with no apologies, and our *environment* is often beyond our control.

What if you were born with all the muscles, skill and quickness to be the fastest skier in the world? The problem is you were born in Jamaica.

What Makes The Difference?

David said in Psalms 139:13-16:

Oh yes, you shaped me first inside, then out;
You formed me in my mother's womb.
I thank you, High God—you're breathtaking.
Body and soul, I am marvelously made!
I worship in adoration—what a creation!
You know me inside and out,

You know every bone in my body:
You know exactly how I was made, bit by bit,
How I was sculpted from nothing into something.
Like an open book, you watched me grow from
conception to birth:
All the stages of my life were spread out before you.
The days of my life all prepared
Before I'd even lived one day.

(THE MESSAGE)

One in 100 Million

Heredity and environment are factors that determine who you are, but the most important factor is your response to them. Do you realize that you have the power to change your environment? If you were born in Jamaica and want to be a skier, you will have to move to where there is snow. When you change your environment you have the potential to change your life, and to fulfill your God-given possibilities. Remember, your potential is God-given. What you do with your potential gives you your identity.

ৡ VI ঽ

Discovering
Your Destiny

What is destiny? Destiny is often a thing that parents bequeath to their children. Like a parent's will to their sons and daughters, destiny can be a fortune or it can contain many unpaid debts.

Usually we think of destiny as being a destination. There are two separate meanings that we use to describe destiny. Primarily, it means a conclusion, an end, or a result. It also means a path or road that takes us to our destination.

Isaiah 30:21 states, "Whether you turn to the right or to the left, your ears will hear a voice behind you, saying, 'This is the way; walk in it.' " And Jeremiah 29:11 states, " 'For I know the plans I have for you,' declares the Lord, 'plans to prosper you and not to harm you, plans to give you hope and a future.' "

In reading Hebrew 11:15-16, we receive a more complete picture of the journey of those who know Christ. "If they had been thinking of the country they had left, they would have had opportunity to return. Instead they were longing for a better country—a heavenly one. Therefore God is not ashamed to be called their God, for he has prepared a city for them."

Destiny is a road. The road we each travel can be good, bad or in-between.

The question we must answer is: Does God determine our destiny or do we? I think the answer is we both do. Remember the painting on the ceiling of the Sistine Chapel in which God is reaching down, and man is reaching up, until their fingers almost touch? It is kind of like that.

Destiny is your will lining up with God's plan. For example, have you ever ridden in bumper cars? When the post on the back of your car makes contact with the ceiling, which is the power source, you go. If somehow you become disconnected, you don't go, and other cars will come and ram you from all over the place. Lining up with God's plan could also be like the luge event in the Olympics; that toboggan must stay on the track. There has never been a winner who jumped the track.

Parents Hold the Power

Parents have a tremendous influence on their children. It's like they unlock a secret door and welcome a certain family power or truth to saturate the next generation with direction and destiny.

For a person who has been given a negative or ungodly road upon which to travel, is it possible to change their destiny? Yes, because by God's grace and a sincere dedication to find God's will for life, their past can be healed. If a miracle does not take place, that person will continue to be affected by the words, examples, vision, spirit, and life's thrust that has been given them by his or her parents. This direction can be secular, ungodly, or spiritual. One great hope that we do have is in knowing that a sincere dedication to the things of God will change the past as well as the future.

Parents do not always have a dream or a clear vision of their son's or daughter's future. The truth is that parents need to bring their children up "in the fear and admonition of the Lord," which helps them set a course that has a godly vision. Parents must talk about the past, and how God brought them through life. They need to talk about their faith and how God honored His word in their decision-making and choices.

When parents pray for their sons and daughters they need not only pray for the small things, but also for the big things that will take miracles to accomplish. Sometimes parents are afraid to pray for those kinds of miracles, in case they don't happen and the young person will lose faith. Do not do that. How else can they ever believe in a destiny if they never see God answer really difficult matters?

Discipline and Destiny

Growing up in South Dakota, I had a friend called Jake. Jake was a real slob. He didn't comb his hair, brush his teeth, or ever wear clean or pressed clothes. One day, however, I beheld a transformed image. What a change!

"Jake," I said, "You really look great, man; you got a haircut and new shoes. What happened?"

"I just kind of felt I should change a little," he replied vaguely.

The truth was that Nadine sat next to him in class, and now he had a goal motivating him to change.

Parents need to talk about challenges, about goals, and about the future. They need to get involved with their son's and daughter's thinking. If you leave all thoughts of the future up to the public schools, television, or their own peers, they will become confused. Children need to hear you say, repeatedly, that you believe in them, that God will guide them, and that prayer does make a difference. Quote to them the encouraging words of the Bible that state, "The steps of a righteous person are ordered of the Lord."

Destiny Has Two Wicked Stepsisters

The first of these is fatalism, as implied in the phrase, "*Que sera sera*," or "There is nothing I can do about this, so I'll just expect the worst."

Let me relate an account that illustrates such an attitude of fatalism: Linda drives into a convenience store. She notices a lady sleeping in the next car. She is sitting there with her hands gripping the back of her neck, with her eyes closed. Linda goes into the store and does her shopping. She comes back out, and notices that the lady is still sitting there. But now her eyes are wide open, with a look of terror on her face.

Linda senses something is wrong, so she goes over and knocks on the window and asks her what is troubling her.

"I have been shot in the back of my head, and my brains are falling out," the lady shouts. "I am trying to hold them in."

Linda runs back in the store and asks them to dial 9-1-1. The emergency crew comes, breaks the window, and notices a wad of biscuit dough, where the lady's hands are on the back of her neck.

What actually happened was a can of biscuit dough that she had purchased got so hot inside the car that it exploded, shooting out of the can, hitting her in the back of the neck. She thought she had been shot, so when she grabbed the back of her head and felt the biscuit dough, she thought it was her brains falling out. Frightened, she passed out. She eventually regained consciousness but just couldn't let her brains fall out.

The Other Wicked Stepsister is Presumption

Presumption says, "God had better come through. He is in charge, so there is nothing I will do about it." In essence, both fatalism and presumption imply that there is nothing to be done about the current situation.

Whenever destiny invites us to cooperate with God in the unfolding of our lives, we are getting close to understanding our ultimate destiny. In a practical sense, our understanding of destiny might compare to what we believe about the Scriptures in the book of James, which states that we need both faith *and* works.

Let us say that my right leg represents my faith in God, and my left leg represents doing those things that make my experiences with faith in God understandable and profitable for the winning of others to Him.

If I only use my faith and never put myself into action, I would only be walking on my right leg, going in circles. If I just do good things, but never truly trust in God or comprehend His miraculous touch on my life, I would only be using my left leg, and I would be going in circles the other direction.

Destiny represents the balance between free will and God's foreknowledge of our life. God's will is not magical fatalism, or blind presumption. The destiny we enjoy and give to our children is that keen sense of reaching out and touching God, who in turn, is reaching out to us to enfold us in His love, and give us direction for our children's lives.

One of the biggest issues that people deal with is knowing what God's will actually *is*. Parents can help their children work through this issue by building trust and confidence into their children as they guide them step-by-step in their daily personal faith in God's plan.

Isaiah 30:21 states, "And thine ears shall hear a word behind thee, saying, 'This is the way, walk ye in it, when ye turn to the right hand, and when ye turn to the left' " (KJV).

One of the great gifts of parents to a son or daughter is helping him or her to define and inhabit their divine God-given destiny. Part of that gift is teaching them how to listen to what God is telling them individually.

Six Vital Declarations of Destiny

1. My destiny is safe from outside circumstances.

Esther 4:14 states, "For if you remain silent at this time, relief and deliverance for the Jews will arise from another place, but you and your father's family will perish. And who knows but that you have come to royal position for such a time as this?"

Despite the fact that it is easy to think that such an arrangement was merely a coincidence, Queen Esther had been placed in the king's palace so that she could save her people. How frequent it is that a completely unrelated event intersects our plans puts us in a different position to meet the critical turning point for the fulfillment of our destiny.

For example, early in our ministry we were positioned to leave a church, in a small community. In the process we received a call from a church in northern California to come candidate as pastors. The day before we had planned to drive to California, I thought it would be good to touch base with that church, and let them know we were still planning on being there the next Sunday. I shall never forget the ego-deflating words, and shock of disappointment, when the person on the other end of the line, said, "Oh, don't come, the congregation voted in Reverend So-and-So last evening."

The years have gone by, and God has directed us in marvelous ways. We soon became aware how merciful God had been to us then, by putting the right persons in that position, thereby leading us in a different direction.

Nothing happens outside of God's notice. If we are submitted to God, He has all time and events in His hands. He never forces us to follow Him, but He makes His will available to us. Our destiny may feel the impact of events both good and bad, but when we are close to God, we can be assured that our destiny is safe.

2. My destiny is safe from people with wicked intent.

People who are up to mischief might try to influence our future. Young people often feel this influential presence, and may even come to a place where they are sure there is no hope. Joseph is probably the best example of this. His brothers were so jealous of him that they tried to permanently do away with him. They eventually sold him as a slave to a caravan that took him to Egypt. It was there that the destiny of all of Israel was affected by Joseph's experience in finding favor with the pharaoh. Later, his brothers came to Egypt looking for work, also bringing their elderly father. And after his father died, Joseph still held explicit faith in God as he confronted his brothers as Genesis 50:19 states,

> *And Joseph said unto them, "Fear not: for am I in the place of God? But as for you, ye thought evil against me; but God meant it unto good, to bring to pass, as it is this day, to save much people alive. Now therefore fear ye not: I will nourish you, and your little ones." And he comforted them, and spake kindly unto them.*

As in Joseph's account, sometimes those with the very worst intentions can help you fulfill your destiny. We have seen some people become angry and bitter to the point of losing the joy of their salvation, and their hope for the future. Perhaps the harshness of a teacher, or the lack of understanding of a parent, causes one's spirit to close and shut out love. But look what Joseph did: He forgave and ministered to his brothers and their families. Not only was his destiny a terrific blessing, but for all generations, the Jewish people still revere and honor this godly man who would not let evil intentions ruin his destiny.

If parents or other family members have wounded you, and the damage is still festering in your spirit, take Joseph's example of forgiveness and wipe out that infection with the most powerful antibiotic of the soul: Genuinely forgive them. Doing so will allow you stay on your road of destiny, and bring strength and guidance to the next generation.

3. My destiny is safe from people who have authority over me.

John 19:10-11 states, "'Do you refuse to speak to me?' Pilot said. 'Don't you realize I have power either to free you or to crucify you?' Jesus answered, 'You would have no power over me if it were not given to you from above.'"

Jesus' destiny was to be fulfilled by Pilot's authority over Him. We don't have to struggle against one's authority. Remember that a person, father, mother, schoolteacher, brother or critic is really a part of the journey. Your destiny is safe from their misuse, and unless you allow it, their authority cannot destroy God's plan for your life. In fact, it often becomes the key to releasing and empowering you to the ultimate joy of your life.

4. My destiny is safe from my own inability.

1 Samuel 14:6 states, "Jonathan said to his young armor-bearer, 'Come, let's go over to the outpost of those uncircumcised fellows. Perhaps the Lord will act in our behalf. Nothing can hinder the Lord from saving, whether by many or by few.'"

What a great example of an almost-naïve faith triumphing over a whole army. First Jonathan set up a fleece that he explained to his armor-bearer. He said, "Come, then; we will cross over toward the men and let them see us. If they say, 'Come up to us,' we will climb up, because that will be our sign that the Lord has given them into our hands."

It turned out that the enemy gave them an invitation to come up. They went up and routed the encampment. Eventually panic struck the whole army, giving Israel a great victory that day.

This may be the moment when God can use us the most. We are safe from our own unimpressiveness. When no one wants to follow us, and we are not sure that *anyone* believes in us, it is God who will work in us and through us.

5. My destiny is safe from my own lack of understanding.

Daniel 3:16-18 relates how three Hebrew children reply to their king's demands:

Shadrach, Meshach, and Abednego replied to the king, "O Nebuchadnezzar, we do not need to defend ourselves before you in this matter. If we are thrown into the blazing furnace, the God we serve is able to save us from it, and He will rescue us from your hand, O king. But even if he does not, we want you to know, O king, that we will not serve your gods or worship the image of gold you have set up."

We know how God protected them, and that Christ Himself appeared in that fiery furnace as their protector.

While in India several years ago, we visited a church on the outskirts of a small village. The sign across the front in Hindi read: Pastor Paul's Church. You see, a pastor by the name of Paul came to this village many years ago from a distant land. He labored, to what seemed by many, in vain. No one came to his church, but he remained faithful. He visited the people when there was sickness; he was with them when members of their family died. He talked to them about his Savior, but no one accepted Christ, and still no one came to his church.

Pastor Paul died after many years of an apparently futile ministry. The people of the village took his body to the edge of town and gave Pastor Paul a nice burial. One by one, people young and old came with an offering to place on his grave. Bringing gifts, they came with tears in their eyes to thank him for coming to their village and demonstrating his God. Each one prayed as Pastor Paul had taught them so many times before, accepting Jesus into their heart, and Pastor Paul's ministry lives on today.

God's time is not always our time, and even when we don't know all the details, our destiny is safe. God's love is unconditional.

6. My destiny is safe from my own past mistakes.

1 Timothy 1: 15-16 states,

Christ Jesus came into the world to save sinners—of whom I am the worst. But for that very reason I was shown mercy so that in me, the worst of sinners, Christ Jesus might display his unlimited patience as an example for those who would believe on him and receive eternal life.

Have you ever made a mistake from which you thought you would never recover?

Author John Trent tells this story:

Some of you will remember a picture taken in Vietnam in 1972. In the foreground children are fleeing their village, which has just been destroyed by napalm. Children are crying, no, they are wailing as they run.

American soldiers are walking behind them. Behind them is blackness where a village once stood.

In the center of the picture is a nine-year-old girl. Her clothes are burned from her body. Her arms are raw and welted from napalm. She is holding them out as if she doesn't dare let them touch her skinny, naked, burned body.

A horrible picture. I remember it as it was flashed across our television screens, and then on the cover of various magazines. Then we forgot the picture. But John Plummer, he couldn't forget! He had been the officer who had organized the raid that destroyed the village. He was a pilot of one of the helicopters responsible for the carnage, the burns, the screams, and the little girl.

Plummer thought the village had been cleared of civilians. But the picture, that terrible picture, ran endlessly like a bad movie through his brain. He began to search for the nine-year-old girl. For 24 years, her picture haunted him, tormented him with unspeakable shame, irrepressible guilt. He had nightmares for years. He turned to alcohol for relief, but the pain never left. He lost his self-respect, his marriage; maybe he would lose his mind.

He had to find peace. So on Veteran's Day in 1996 he went to the Vietnam Memorial in Washington, D.C. He watched as one of the speakers stepped to the microphone. He began to tremble with emotion. It was the nine-year-old girl, only now she was 33. She had come to the memorial to lay a wreath and to speak.

Her name was Kim. Phan Thi Kim Phuc. She told of the pain, then and now. She told how thousands had died, how many had lost parts of their bodies.

Lives had been destroyed, but no one had taken their picture. Then she said, "But I have forgiven the men who bombed my village."

Finally, John heard the words that he had needed for over two decades. He jumped to his feet and started to run, and as he got closer he began to shout, "I'm sorry, I'm so sorry, I am sorry." Tears are streaming down his face. Then Kim said, "It's all right, I forgive you."

They only had two minutes together before her police escort took Kim away. They wept, and embraced one another. John and Kim had started from opposite sides of the war to bridge this deep and terrible gulf between enemies. In that embrace they made peace not only with each other, but with the past. Today they are good friends.[1]

You may live with dark and devastating memories of the past: past sins, past mistakes, including sins that were forced upon you. The loss of a child in a wreck, in a car you were driving, can be a haunting memory. Or, as a child you may have played with matches catching the house on fire. Perhaps, your mother told you often that you would never amount to anything.

God's love is not conditional. He does not say, "I will stop loving you, guiding you, reaching out for you because you made a mistake." Instead, He says, "I even loved you while you were sinning." Your destiny is safe.

Destiny is not superstition, predestination, fatalism, blind bondage, magic, accidental eventuation, a plaything for a powerful force, a chance, or a blind impulse. Instead, it is about foreordination and free will. It is when God's foreordained plan and our free will join hands and travel the same road. This can only be accomplished when 1) we have a personal, practical day-by-day relationship with Jesus Christ, and 2) we yield to the idea that all things are in Gods hands.

We should not feel impotent before God and assume that we are mere atoms in the universe. God created us and destined us to make a difference.

I don't know what your destiny may be. However, I do have a good idea what the negative effects of life's events can do. I also know what the positive effects can have upon your life. You can affect your world as you discover your destiny and travel on that road.

Remember these six declarations of *your* destiny.

- Your destiny is safe from outside circumstances.
- Your destiny is safe from people with wicked intent.
- Your destiny is safe from people who have authority over you.
- Your destiny is safe from your own inability.
- Your destiny is safe from your own lack of understanding.
- Your destiny is safe from your own past mistakes.

There is a stirring account of a small monk, just five feet tall, who went to the local coliseum one day in the fourth century. He found himself seated near the top, with 80,000 other people in the stands. The venue for the day provided gladiators contesting with one another for life and death. After the small monk saw one gladiator kill another, he jumped out of his seat, ran down to the edge, jumped over it and into the dust of the coliseum. He stood as tall as he could, held up his arms, and shouted at the top of his voice, "Forebear. In the name of Jesus, forebear."

The crowd started booing and yelling at him to leave and let the games go on.

But the monk was persistent; he would not leave. Finally the crowd began yelling, "Get him out of here! Get him out of here!" One of the gladiators came over and with the flat of his sword slapped him across the face and knocked him down. But the monk jumped to his feet and held up his hands, shouting, "In the name of Jesus, forebear." The crowd became more irritated, and started yelling, "Kill him! Kill him!"

The gladiator came back and ran his sword through the monk's chest. The monk fell to the ground, and knowing that he was dying, struggled to his feet and barely spoke his final words, "Forebear. Forebear. In the name of Jesus…"

There was now a deathly silence that settled over the scene. Quietly, a man near the top of the coliseum got up and walked out. Another individual walked out, then another, then a whole row, then an entire section. Very shortly the whole coliseum was emptied. And there was never another game of that kind held in the coliseum.

It takes people with courage and a will that is linked to God's plan to follow their destiny. Destiny is not history; it is the road that lies ahead.

Here are a few good questions to ask yourself when determining your destiny:

1. What is your greatest desire? (See Psalms 37:4.)
2. What is the one thing that stirs you most? (See Psalms 69:9.)
3. What gifts flow naturally from your life? (See Romans 12:4-6.)
4. Does the Spirit witness peace with your spirit in this direction?
5. Do Christian friends and leaders verify your steps?
6. Do you feel you can give your life to this direction?
7. Has God helped you overcome obstacles?[2]

❧ VII ❧

Vision

What does it mean to have a vision of the future? How can parents help their children develop a dream? What are some of the attitudes that can blur a vision?

Dietrich Bonhoeffer, a German theologian and one of the Christian martyrs of the Nazi holocaust had gone a long way by the age of 39. He had completed his education; taught in colleges; and been a pastor and leader wherever he went. He was an intelligent theologian with a special touch of God upon his life that directed his every step.

He knew that Hitler's extermination of the Jews was terribly wrong, even though the liberal branch of his church kept quiet about the Holocaust. He became a leader in the resistance, and had even gone so far as planning the death of Hitler.

He was eventually arrested and placed in prison just weeks before his own wedding. He suffered greatly while in prison for two years. He felt sorry for himself and for the shame he had brought upon his well-respected family. Knowing what his end might be, he even contemplated suicide. In his book, *Letters and Papers from Prison,*[1] he states that without a clear vision of God's plans for him, and a keen purpose for his life, he could never have gone on. He was killed by Hitler's henchmen, but he died with a vision of Jesus, and a picture of an overcoming church in his mind.[2]

To dream is "to conceive in one's mind something that isn't, and believe that it shall be." It is like building a house, or developing a business, or dreaming about the future of your family.

A vision is "the power of perceiving something not actually present to the eye, whether by supernatural insight, imagination, or by clear thinking."

I have found that within many of God's promises lies the foundation for a vision. "Seek ye first the Kingdom of God, and His righteousness; and all these things shall be added unto you" (Matthew 6:33 KJV).

I have noticed that the people who have a definite vision as to where they are going most often get to their destination. The people who have a vision of their future are happier; they are more exciting to be around; they are more successful; and they are more passionate.

Aim at something and you are sure to hit it.

Imaginations

As a child I would dream that I could sing—I mean really sing. That dream would have been a real miracle because I've never really had that talent. Later on in life, I dreamt that somehow I would come into a good deal of money, justifying it by not making it just a selfish dream: I would imagine building churches all over the country. I must say, that too would have been a miracle because no one in our family has ever had a lot of money. But, neither of these was ever part of a God-given vision for my life.

Imagination can be good, but it is different from a vision for the future, or a life's dream. Unless our imaginations are sanctified by the Holy Spirit, they can destroy us.

Look at the condition of the earth just before the flood. "Every imagination of the thoughts of his [mankind's] heart was only evil continually" (Genesis 6:5 KJV).

Jeremiah 7:24 states, "They went backward not forward when they walked in the counsel and in the imagination of their evil hearts." Jeremiah 11:8 states, "They followed evil when they listened to their imaginations." And Jeremiah 3:17 states, "And all nations shall be gathered in to Jerusalem, neither shall they walk any more in the imagination of their evil hearts" (KJV).

Imagination almost always connotes carnal thinking or planning. It is amazing how people will stop listening to the voice of God coming through their gifts and visions to follow their own fantasies. Pornography is an example of this. I have talked to scores of men at retreats, men both young and old. I have learned of this diabolical addiction that is ruining marriage after marriage. If your imagination has turned into these kinds of fantasies, your marriage partner will never be good enough for you.

"Where there is no vision the people perish" (Proverbs 29:18). God's promises do not create fantasies or carnal imaginations. Within every promise of God's lies the foundation of a vision.

The Lord had said to Abram, "Leave your country, your people and your father's household and go to the land I will show you. I will make you into a great nation and I will bless you; I will make your name great, and you will be a blessing. I will bless those who bless you, and whoever curses you I will curse; and all peoples on earth will be blessed through you" (Genesis 12:1-3).

Can you imagine how Abraham allowed those promises to become his guiding passion? Remember that he had no children, yet he was to become the father of a great nation. God spared his nephew Lot through Abraham's passion to see his dream fulfilled.

Finally, Isaac was born. Now Abraham's dream had become so vivid, his faith so strong, that when he was asked to offer Isaac as a sacrifice on the altar, he didn't even question God. I cannot imagine responding to a request like that if God were to ask me to sacrifice one of my grandsons. I remember the anguish my wife and I had when our daughter Lynne and her husband Jonathan went to Israel to minister in an Arab boys' school on the West Bank. It was so far away. We felt helpless when she told us that one day just as she left the market a bomb exploded.

We must remember that Abraham was a human being. He let his vision turn into imagination when he denied that Sara was his wife, saying that she was his sister. Thankfully his vision clarified as God began to fulfill His promises one step at a time. He began to pour those promises into Isaac his son. When Abraham's vision was fulfilled, God's promises became the guiding light for his son, and then his grandsons, and each generation that would keep the covenant God made.

We can recount many great people of God, as God's promises became the foundation for their dream: Moses, Jeremiah, Daniel, the disciples, Ruth, Esther, and Martin Luther, Billy Graham, and many more.

To really accomplish God's plans in each area of our lives we must have a vision.

What is your vision for your marriage, your mate, your children, and your grandchildren? What is your dream for your job, your ministry, or your church?

We have a great privilege as parents to help lay the foundation for our sons and daughters to develop a life vision for them to pursue.

Attitudes That Blur Vision

1. **A critical spirit:** It denies the move of faith in one's heart, and closes an individual's ability to communicate trust and hope.
2. **Perfectionism:** It is afraid to take a chance. It says, "This step may have some ragged edges and I won't know how to handle it. If this doesn't work out just right, people will think I was wrong."
3. **Fear, doubt and unbelief:** Fear and doubt usually start out as honest emotions. They evolve into self-protection, and eventually lead to the ultimate denial that produces unbelief. It is like a small snowball at the top of the mountain that turns into a gigantic life-destroying monster the farther it travels. It not only picks up speed, it eventually turns into an avalanche destroying everything in its path. Deal with your fears and doubts lest you later have to deal with a lack of faith.
4. **A super-spiritual attitude:** Frankly, no one likes a know-it-all. Sometimes we are especially blessed in a certain area, and if we are not very careful, spiritual success can go to our head, like any other success. We will compare ourselves to others who have not experienced what we have. In doing so, we make them feel less than children of God. Super-success in spiritual areas is often harder to live with than a failure or two along the way.

What Does A God-Given Vision Do For You?

1. A vision gives purpose.

Viktor Frankl, an Austrian psychologist who survived the death camps of Nazi Germany, made a very significant discovery. He found within himself the capacity to rise above a frightening and humiliating ordeal. He also observed his fellow prisoners, becoming intrigued by the fact that a few of them survived.

At first he thought the reason for their survival might be health, vitality, intelligence, or perhaps, survival skills. He eventually came to the conclusion that none of these was primarily responsible. The single most compelling factor was a sense of vision. The conviction of those who were to survive was that they had a mission to complete, some important work left to do.

It may have been the compelling desire to see one's family, a wife, or a newborn baby. There was an imminent, future-oriented vision that became a passion in each of their lives. Perhaps Solomon knew this when he wrote, "Where there is no vision, the people perish" (Proverb 29:18 KJV).

The power of vision is incredible. Children with future-focused role models perform far better scholastically, and are drastically better at handling the challenges of life.[3]

Vision is the best manifestation of a creative imagination. When a young person develops a passion for a dream or purpose in life it becomes a fantastic force for success.

More than anything else, vision affects the choices we make and the way we spend our time. If our vision is limited, if it doesn't go beyond the Friday night ball game, or the next television show, we tend to make our choices based only on what is before us. We react to whatever is urgent—the impulse of the moment, our mood, limited options, and other people's priorities. The feelings we have about our decisions will vacillate and fluctuate, changing from day to day.

When any people, society, family, man or woman lacks a revelation (divine insight) from God, they will wander in a wasteland. People who have a vibrant vision of what God wants them to be, or what they should do, develop a directed sense of purpose.

When we think of Moses, we think of a man who had an unbelievable drive to take his people to the Promised Land.

When we think of Martin Luther King Jr., some of us can hear that vibrant voice saying, "I have a dream." Think of Mother Teresa, whose great purpose in life was to feed and clothe the downtrodden and homeless in India.

Purpose tells a person who he or she is, and it actually tells us all why we exist. When we develop purpose it guides us to whom we will marry; how we earn and spend our money; and how we are going to raise and educate our children.

With a clearly defined purpose, even the tragic and most difficult events in our lives do not sink our ship. Purpose becomes a part of our very being and is a symbol of God's healing power in our lives. We are then able to pass through the darkest night.

I have a policy of sending my book, *Generational Legacy: Breaking the Curse, Starting the Blessing* to prisoners when requested by family members.

A few weeks after sending the book to James in a state correctional facility, I received a letter saying, "I now know why I am in jail. I followed in the footsteps of so many members of my family. But for the first time I feel free. I took the steps suggested in your book for removing a generational curse." Later he wrote, "I have started to write a book on recovery."

As we continued to correspond I could see how James was finding purpose for living, even though he was still in prison. He was developing a vision for helping those much like himself. A miracle takes place when we stop looking inside our own darkness for help and instead get a vision of whom we can be in Christ. It will cause us to walk taller, jump higher, run faster, and win more than we ever thought possible.

Empty dreams only bring discouragement and frustration. If someone doesn't affirm our dreams, giving us a reason to continue following our vision, we begin to shrivel and dry up. Again, as the book of Proverbs states, "Without purpose, the people perish."

2. Vision keeps us focused.

Several years ago Bill, a young student at Eugene Bible College in Eugene, Oregon, where I was an administrator, started dropping by my office. Graduation was coming, and I knew that he had been looking for a church at which to serve as a youth pastor. His folks were pastors and he knew that this direction was their hope for him. On this day he seemed rather down, and I sensed he was discouraged. We talked and considered some options for him, and I felt we just weren't getting anywhere.

I said, "Bill if you could take the next year and do whatever you wanted and didn't have to worry about making a living, what would you do?" His face lit up like a 500-watt light bulb.

He jumped up and started telling me that when he was in high school he was very good in mathematics. One day a teacher asked him if he would like to tutor some junior high students who were falling behind in their math class. He got even more excited as he began to tell me of that experience. He remembered, "We started at the beginning of their particular class, and as I met with them, they really seemed to get it." He shared how their grades went up, and how they had all come to him, thanking him for being such a good teacher and helping them so much.

I asked Bill, "Do you suppose this is your calling? Maybe you should be a math teacher. Teachers with a godly passion are really needed, and this could be a great ministry."

He was still worried about what his folks might think. I encouraged him to talk to them about it; he might be really surprised. He did. And they suggested he pray about it, and look into going on to another school to get his teaching certificate.

I remember the excitement in his life as he found just the school, and went on to become a math teacher. Bill might have been an adequate youth pastor, and eventually a senior pastor, but he was a phenomenal math teacher.

A real vision is the vehicle of God's communication with a person. That which God sees in secret He will reward openly.

3. A vision is a clear mental picture of the future.

It is not always perfectly clear and understandable, but the farther you walk, the clearer it becomes. Fathers and mothers must understand the power of having a vision: a vision for your own life, and a vision that you can pass on to your children, which they will use to build into their lives as a source of power and strength, direction and purpose.

My brother-in-law, Gerald Wood is a gifted wood carver. He explained to me that he always envisions the finished carving before the piece is finished, and usually before he ever starts carving it he has a clear mental photograph of where he is going.

A few years ago he was commissioned by Marie Smith to carve a dove for the baptistry in honor of her late husband, Pastor Frank W. Smith. Pastor Smith had pastored at this church for 37 years, and Gerald wanted it done right. But he just could not see it. Six months went by and the people at the church wondered why the dove was not finished. Finally Gerald realized that the vision was not his, it was Marilyn Longs', who had drawn the original dove. It was then that he decided to load up all his carving equipment, the piece of wood that was to become a dove, and drive to her home.

They sat at the kitchen table, while she walked him through step-by-step of her vision of the dove. He would carve and she would tell him where and how much. When it was completed the dove was a beautiful work of art. But only after Marilyn's vision was clearly communicated could he see it come alive.

As mothers and fathers, sometimes we must literally do this. Stand waiting and ready for God to reveal His plan for each of our children. We can then be confident as we love, pray, encourage, and teach our children to be what God would have them to be. It takes patience and sometimes a lot of hard work to communicate our vision to our family.

Some people may think that having such a mental portrait is a little mystical, and maybe too far out. But for those who have that kind of vision, it is as real as the finished product. Vision focuses on what does not yet exist, but will come to pass as you pursue it.

A godly parent must have a vision for the future: a vision for home, family, each child, and ministry, laying a foundation that will help his or her children walk into the future with confidence and faith. This Scripture from the Old Testament is just as important today as when it was spoken to the children of Israel.

> These commandments that I give you today are to be upon your hearts. Impress them on your children. Talk about them when you sit at home and when you walk along the road, when you lie down, and when you get up. Tie them as symbols on your hands and bind them on your foreheads. Write them on the doorframes of your houses and on your gates (Deuteronomy 6:6-9).

4. A vision directs one's heart toward heaven.

True north is the magnetic pole. One can't get any more northern. It is the point to which all compasses are set.

If our vision is based on illusion, we make choices that are not based on true north principles. Our vision degenerates to platitudes and other people's ideas. We can even become cynical, not trusting our dream any more. God's word, not social mores, is our true north.

Consider the images that are projected by the media: cynicism, skepticism, violence, indulgence, fatalism, and materialism. Our world would have us to believe that only bad news is important news.

How could the apostle Paul continue on, after trials, persecution, disappointments, and loss? Yet he declared passionately, "I press toward the mark for the prize of the high calling of God, in Christ Jesus" (Philippians 3:14 KJV).

The Passion of Vision

The passion of vision gives us energy that comes with purpose and principles. It taps into the core of who we really are and what our life is all about. It defines the legacy that we will leave.

When passion is coupled with a vision, it redefines the common man. It clarifies purpose, gives us direction, and empowers us to go beyond our natural resources.

This passion becomes such a motivating force in our lives that it literally becomes our DNA. Everything we do and decision we make is affected by the passion of our vision. Who we are is defined by our vision with passion.

Join passionate vision to God's plan for your life; the presence of Christ in your heart; and the leading of the Holy Spirit. You have a fire that will transcend all human expectations.

Solomon gave us the key to this concept when he said, "Where there is no vision, the people perish" (Proverbs 29:18 KJV). The New International Version is even clearer, "Where there is no revelation, the people cast off restraint." In other words, unless you and your family have a very definite sense of purpose, direction, and parameters, you will all live according to your own choices and will just naturally be lured away by cultural and carnal desires.

Help Your Child Become A Vision Maker

1. Develop a plan before your son or daughter is born.

This plan should help you answer the question, "How will I relate to my child?" The key is that your child will be able to relate to you, believe you, admire you, trust you, and want to be with you.

If you don't decide the vision for your child, someone else will decide for you. Your ideals and goals are not necessarily what the world considers valuable, and your son or daughter is not high on the world's list of priorities.

2. Don't despair a child who is a dreamer.

In fact, it is positive to help him develop a keen imagination. Nearly every invention, every architectural masterpiece, every classic work of literature, and every great drama, was first in someone's mind as a dream. The dream became a reality as it consumed that person's life.

The story is told about a group touring Disney World in Florida, of which someone observed, "It is too bad that Walt Disney never got to see this great place in its finished state." His son, who was leading the tour, responded, "Oh, but sir, he *did* see it."

3. A child must be encouraged to put a vision into words and objectively talk about it.

The third trait becomes a gift as the young person grows. Never tell your child that his or her dream is only a fantasy that will never happen. Listen to the dream, dream with them. Help them to know the difference between impossibilities, silly fantasies, or just pretend, and visions that are not seen now, but will be. Provide them with autobiographies of people who accomplished their dreams. Encourage them to read and plan times of open discussion without ever belittling or making light of even childish dreams. Share with them the vision or dreams that you had as a child.

4. Help your son or daughter develop a good attitude.

Model a good attitude. Be positive. Pray with your child when she has big needs. Pray for people and circumstances that demand faith. Expect miracles. Don't be afraid to believe God for the unbelievable. Talk about the answers that come. Your consistent faith will become her faith. Your prayers will be echoed in your child's heart for years. I find myself praying almost the same words that I heard my father use in prayer. I would like to think that I pray with the same faith that my mom and dad enjoyed. Your attitude about most everything in life will have a startling effect upon your children.

5. Teach your child how to win *and* lose.

You can do this by playing games, and arranging group sporting activities. Don't beat the socks off the small fry in every activity, but don't intentionally lose every contest either.

I am now at the place with my grandsons where they can beat me at most any active sport. I have vowed that when one of them beats me at golf, it will be because he has really won. I know it won't be long, but *they* know that until then, each is in a fierce battle. Playing together can be one of the most healthy parent-child encounters possible.

6. Help your child develop at least one skill.

Everyone should have one thing they are just a little above average in doing. Send them to a competent music teacher. Enroll them in a little league team that has the very best coach. Do not take any shortcuts when it comes to developing skills in your children. If you notice that they are not living up to a talent or gift, it is your responsibility to see that they get the proper help.

Several years ago I noticed that my grandsons were not really reading like I believed they should. I offered to give them a penny a page for whatever they read, except school texts. They had to keep a record by giving me the name of the book and number of pages. It eventually became very costly for me. One year I gave Ryan over 100 dollars, and each of the other boys was soon doing the same. But it paid off. Today these all-American boys will almost always have a book that goes everywhere they go.

7. Make certain that your children have been given Bible knowledge and a spiritual foundation.

Read the Bible together in short spurts, talk about it, discuss it, ask questions and answer their questions.

Make sure that they are in a good Bible class, particularly if they attend a public school. Encourage them to attend a youth group that doesn't just play games, but talks about current issues and contemporary problems, and gives spiritual insights. This means you must take your children to a Bible-believing church and be there with them.

A Mission Statement

Many people have found that one of the most helpful and directive exercises that they have done is write a mission statement. This can be an open connection to what your vision is telling you, where you should go in life, and how you can relate to true north.

We each live three lives:

1. A public life where we interact with society

2. A private life in which we are alone with very close family members
3. A deep inner life—our most significant life

The third one is where we connect and commune with God. This is where we come to grips with the gifts and values that have been bestowed upon us. It is here where our free will and God's foreknowledge are linked together. This is where our passion for service comes out, and we begin to grasp who we are, and what we must do.

Mission statements that come out of public or private thinking will never access your deep inner core and God's empowerment.

Solomon gave us the key to this concept: Where there is no vision the people perish. Or, where there is no revelation, people cast off all restraint. Apply this to your future. Where are you going? Unless you have a very definite sense of purpose, direction, and parameters, you will live according to your own choices, will, and imagination.

A Mission Statement for Your Life

To properly write and use your mission statement, remember:

- Your mission statement represents the deepest and best within you.
- It springs out of your gifts. You have a sense of excitement and well-being because it represents the true you.
- It deals with a vision that has been growing in your life for a long time.
- You sincerely believe that you can place this statement over every decision, every relationship, and know that if you obey its leading you will never be ashamed.

- It becomes a living testament of your goals, ambitions, and God-empowered gifts.

Vision is a picture of your future. It keeps you on course. If the camera is not in focus, the picture is blurry and you may not distinguish God's direction for your life. It is important to write your vision down so that it will be before you at all times. Your decisions will always be made with your vision in mind.

> *Then the Lord replied: Write down the revelation and make it plain on tablets so that a herald may run with it. For the revelation awaits an appointed time; it speaks of the end and will not prove false. Though it linger, wait for it; it will certainly come and will not delay (Habakkuk 2:2-3).*

Review

Perhaps now you can answer the following questions:

- What does it mean to have a vision for your future?
- How can parents help their children to have a dream?
- What are some of the attitudes that can blur a vision?

ৡ VIII ৡ

The Family Blessing

Part I

I spoke on the subject of the Family Blessing at a retreat in Nebraska. Following my session, a man in his early 40s approached me with a very serious look on his face. I sensed something I had said about families concerned him, so I asked him if he had children.

"Yes," he answered.

"Have you blessed your children?" I asked

"I don't know how to," he answered softly.

Just as he said that, I looked past him for just a moment and noticed an older version of this man.

"Is that your father?" I asked.

He turned and said very quickly, "Yes, this is my dad."

I was very sure that he had just revealed to me his difficulty, so I asked, "Did your father ever bless you?"

With tears beginning to well up in his eyes, he replied, "Oh no, he never did."

I turned to the father and said, "Dad, I believe it's time you really blessed your son."

The son fell suddenly on his knees in front of his father, and one of the most emotional and blessed moments I have ever witnessed took place. The father began to affirm his son as a man, as an honest and godly man, as a son in whom he was so enormously proud. Then he prayed. The son stood and for several minutes, they hugged, wept and laughed. I shall never forget the laughter. It was as if the pent-up emotions from the past were released and they were both free.

Later the son revealed to me that he had always wished his dad would have told him when it was that he became a man, and blessed him.

This and many similar events caused me to realize that something was missing in our Christian Protestant culture.

My First Bar Mitzvah

Our daughter Lynne attended high school in West Des Moines, Iowa. One of her best friends was a Jewish girl of whom our family became very fond. One day she asked if Lynne and her family would like to come to the synagogue to witness her brother's Bar Mitzvah. We of course were delighted and honored with the invitation. The experience literally changed my life.

This beautiful ceremony began with three generations being called up to the front to stand behind what I would call an altar. First, the grandfather read Scriptures from a rolled up Torah. He then handed the Torah to his son, who in turn read more Scriptures. The father of the young man then recited a blessing, which included his thanks to God for removing the burden of being responsible for his son's sins. Then the father handed the scroll to his son, the celebrant, who started his speech with the words, "Today, I am a man." Then he read more Scriptures, and quoted at length, from memory, very meaningful precepts that encompassed what this moment was all about. When he concluded his talk, he suddenly threw back his head, stood as tall as he could, and said in a very positive and clear voice, "Today, I am proud to be a Jew." I wanted to cheer, or at the least say a loud "Amen," but I restrained myself. It was an unforgettable moment.

The generational blessing became very clear that day. I knew that I must teach this age-old truth to as many people as I could for as many years as I had left.

The Historical Background of the Blessing

Most cultures in the world have some form of a rite of passage, which occurs at a similar stage as the Bar Mitzvah in the lives of their children.

Some African cultures have a rite of passage that includes all boys in a village who arrive at the age of puberty at the same time. On a certain day, the men of the village suddenly disappear. A short time later, a group of fierce strangers (the boys' fathers and uncles in disguise) descends on the village. The terrified boys run to their mothers, but their mothers cannot protect them, and the strangers drag them away to the forest.

For the next several days or weeks, the boys undergo a spiritual boot camp. They are smeared with mud and ashes. They are given little food, and not allowed to sleep more than a few hours at a time. The boys must prove their physical and spiritual strength by enduring discomfort without complaint and by submitting to insults and humiliation without protest. At the same time, their captors begin instructing the boys in what it means to be a man. They relate stories about the great men of their nation. They talk about the tests the boys will face and tell them how to behave when the time comes.

The Aborigines have a custom called the walkabout. As a boy grows up, he learns the skills of survival by watching and helping the older men of his group. He learns how to locate food and water, how to find his way in a trackless desert, and how to make the tools and weapons he needs.

When he feels he has mastered these skills, the boy leaves his group and goes off by himself to an isolated area, walking about, for six months to a year. He might not encounter another human being during the entire time. A walkabout is a hard test. There are no second chances. Accidents, mistakes, and bad luck claim many lives. However, if the boy has learned the lessons of survival, he will return to his group, confident in his own skills, prepared to take on a man's role, for he has passed the test of mankind.

In some tribal ceremonies, boys roll stones downhill, racing them to the bottom, hoping to grow into fleet-footed warriors.

At age of maturity, members of Karimo Jong, a Ugandan tribe, learn spearing, cooking, and the eating of an ox.

For centuries when young Jews reach the age of 13, the Bar Mitzvah, (*son of the commandment*) or Bat Mitzvah (*daughter of the commandment*) is celebrated. This marks the end of childhood and the beginning of the period of young manhood or womanhood. It is a significant break and introduction to maturity, where the young person begins to assume a new position in the community. He or she will accept new privileges and responsibilities, and will now be called to account for his or her own actions. This event allows the father and mother a way to say, "I no longer recognize you as a child; the status is now changed, and you are an adult."

By 13, a boy's vow is considered valid and is held to it. He is brought to an elder rabbi of the community and is blessed and prayed for at this time.

Tradition Tells Us

Tradition tells us that: Abraham rejected idol worship when he was 13. At 13, Jacob received the blessing of the firstborn from his father Isaac. Jacob's son Joseph was sold into slavery in Egypt when he was 13. David was 13 when he slew the Philistine giant, Goliath. Solomon became king at the age of 13. Jesus was in the temple at the age of 12.

What Is the Blessing?

There is something inside of every person who longs for a blessing from their parents. As the firstborn son, Esau understood and longed for the blessing from his father. Jacob and his mother were willing to lie and deceive to get this blessing.

In the Hebrew, "to bless" comes from the word *baruch*. *Baruch* literally means, "to kneel down before someone." The primary connotation of this word is "to empower, to prosper." There is a Jewish maxim that says, "The father's blessing builds the child's house."

What It Means Not to Bless

Could it be possible, that to *not* bless would be to disempower a son or daughter? Let us explore this idea just a little more. When a child is blessed, he or she is empowered to prosper. What really happens when a child is blessed? First, we must consider the word, "to prosper," which means to thrive, to do well, or to succeed. With a blessing, prosperity is allowed in many areas not just financially:

1. **Marriage**—In the good times or in the hard times their marriage will thrive.
2. **Children**—They will not always be perfect, but the blessing will empower them in so many different ways.
3. **Finances**—They may never be millionaires, but in the wisdom of the ages, the providential hand of God will provide an adequate living.
4. **Health**—There is no promise of absolute freedom from physical problems, but a positive power of faith will sustain them even in their most trying times.

5. **Career**—When destiny is determined by a partnership with God, prosperity can mean everything from deep satisfaction to what becomes our necessary wealth.
6. **Relationships**—This is one of the greatest parts of the blessing. It helps to cultivate such relationships with others that they may be challenged to enjoy the same blessing in their own lives.

Remember Esau, the son who didn't get the blessing. If we follow his lineage, the Edomites, for many generations, we find that it didn't prosper. They were never a powerful people, and their enemies frequently overran them. On the other hand, the Israelite descendants of Jacob—the son who was blessed—prospered greatly.

The same principle holds true for modern families. Children whose parents have blessed them tend to prosper for many generations. While the families whose parents actively curse them, or leave an unresolved wound tend to have very serious problems for generations.

The Blessing Opens the Door to Prosperity

1. It is a *spiritual act of obedience* to God's plan for the family to continue in the love and knowledge of God.
2. It is a *psychological knowledge* that one's identity and destiny are determined by obedience of a family and to God who loves you.
3. It is verified by the *physical act of hearing* the words and having them confirmed in your heart with a lifelong commitment to *fulfilling* a dream for life.

The Positive, The Negative

To grasp the wonderful connotation of the Blessing we need to see the Curse or the non-Blessing. In the New Testament, the Greek word for "blessing" is *eulogio*, from which we derive the word "eulogy." It means "to speak well of," or "to express praise." James 3:10 speaks of the opposite. "Out of the same mouth comes praise and cursing. My brothers this should not be." When we give a blessing to our children, they receive a certain form of strength or guidance. If we do not bestow this strength or guidance upon them, in essence we disempower them for the obstacles that will confront them. Proverbs 26:2 says, "Like a fluttering sparrow or a darting swallow, an undeserved curse does not come to rest." I sincerely believe that a blessing protects individuals from an undeserved curse coming to rest upon them.

Uncaring Words That Last For Generations

"You are stupid." "Ugly." "You were a mistake." "You will never amount to anything." "Damn you."

Sinful words always set into motion a downward spiral of repetitive pain that can last for generations. (This subject is covered extensively in Chapter II.)

When I began to understand this principle, I understood the Scripture in Exodus 20:6, which talks about, "visiting the sins of the fathers upon the children to the third and fourth generation." I also understood why they were encouraged not only to confess their personal sins, but to confess the sins of their father (Leviticus 26:40 and Nehemiah 1:6). The proxy confession does not release the fathers from their sins. It releases the next generation from the sins of the father who has them bound in a familial sense of idolatry. Sinful acts by one generation can set into motion a downward spiral of repetitive pain as well as an act or attitude of idolatry. Anything in life that becomes a guiding principle becomes idolatry if it takes us away from the peace and presence of God.

What the Blessing Does

In talking about Blessings and Curses, we are not talking about flattery or profanity. These are deep and life-affecting issues that go with us for life. The Blessing does and is many things for the recipient:

1. It releases one from childhood to adulthood.
2. It is a major commitment of gender identity and godly commitment to sexual purity. It could be possible that those confused about their gender identity are so because a father, or some other authority figure in their life, abused them sexually and placed a curse upon them.
3. It is a calling forth of positive character qualities.
4. It might be a reminder of prophetic words spoken about or to the son or daughter in one's early years.
5. It involves specific and personal blessings by the father and mother to the son or daughter.
6. It opens a very wide door for the son or daughter to forgive the mother or father.

Likewise, the parent ought to express forgiveness if there are unresolved conflicts.

It is impossible to forgive someone toward whom you are still locked in idolatry. Your identity is always the issue when forgiveness is at stake. Unforgiveness is always idolatry because it continues to authorize another person to tell you who you are and to send you hurting from that message.

In talking to men from all walks of life including those who have become pornography addicts, sexual abusers, wounded, pathetic human-doers instead of human beings, I found that they usually never had a father after which to model real manhood, so they continued in his sin.

1 Corinthians 10:13-14 states, "There hath no temptation taken you but such as is common to man; but God is faithful who will not suffer you to be tempted above that you

are able, but will with the temptation also make a way to escape, that you may be able to bear it. *Wherefore my dearly beloved, flee from idolatry*" (italics added).

We must help our children establish their true identity: "I am released to be whom God intended me to be. Free from dependence and idolatry. He is my source."

The Next Steps in Life

The blessing is the answer for different phases in one's life, which include:

1. High School

Tom and Arlene had heard me talk about the parental blessing and its tremendous importance to our children. They eventually introduced the subject to their son and his wife, and had them read my first book, *Generational Legacy*. The parents decided to invite all of their family to their son Nathan's blessing. The daughter-in-law's father was a pastor, and when he first heard about the blessing, he responded by declaring that this was strictly Old Testament teaching. However, he was encouraged to read the book and pray about it. He did and subsequently became very enthused about the Blessing, anxious to be part of the ceremony. He was there to give a grandfather's blessing. He also warmed to the idea of giving his grandson a significant symbol of the blessing. Following a tremendous blessing, he then placed around the shoulders of his grandson a beautiful prayer shawl, which he had purchased.

The next day a few of the boy's friends became upset with him and literally knocked him down, beating him quite badly. He later said, "As I was lying there on the ground I remembered that my family had just declared that I was now a man. I decided that I didn't have to play their childish games. So I refused to fight back." The exciting part of the story is that within a few days one of the boys apologized and accepted Christ into his life. Then a short time later another one accepted Christ. Nathan is now in his second year of college, still serving the Lord in a strong way.

2. Events that could be the source of great resentment

I met Jack at a men's retreat in Iowa. I had talked about the influence of fathers, how they provided identity and destiny, and about how every young man needed a dad to keep him from following the example of other guys who were trying to find out who they were. Fathers should teach their sons about sexual pitfalls, pornography, and other temptations that will come their way.

Jack shared how his dad died when he was thirteen, and he missed him desperately. He explained that he had never been blessed, told that he was loved, appreciated, or given any sense of direction or worth. Jack was led into pornography and for the next 10 years, it became a constant part of his life. Now he was married and it was ruining his marriage.

He ran out into the parking lot as I was leaving the retreat, shouting, "Pastor Dan, help me, please, help me."

I prayed for him. Then I believe God directed me to say, "Jack since you don't have a father, may I be your father for a few moments."

"Oh yes," he said.

Like a father, I began to bless him. We asked for forgiveness, for purity, for inner cleansing and peace. As the presence of God surrounded us, I noticed a visible transformation occurring. He was smiling, laughing, and crying all at the same time. As I drove back to the city, my heart ached for all the boys and girls in the world who were missing a mom or a dad and needed to be blessed at just the right time.

3. College

Accounts are coming to me of young people who were blessed in their early teens and are now in college. They and their parents tell me that they could have been sucked into temptation and desperation, but they are sailing through triumphantly because they know who they are and whom they serve.

Jackie was at the end of the first term. It was one week until finals and she knew she must hit the books. Several of her friends were taking the same exam very lightly. She asked why they weren't studying.

One of the girls said, "Sandy has this test from last year and it has all the answers. Jackie, you might just as well join us and save yourself a lot of unnecessary study."

Jackie related that even when she thought of cheating, the words of her father's blessing kept coming to her. "Jackie, one thing about you is that we can always trust you. You never let a dishonest idea or a crooked thought ever take root in your life. We will never have to worry about your decision to lie, or cheat, or deceive another person. Jackie, you must know how extremely proud we are of you. We love you so much."

The interesting part of Jackie's story was that Sandy had the wrong test answers and most of the other girls flunked the exam.

4. Marriage

In a time when Christian marriages equal non-Christian marriages with regard to their failure, our young people need something special inserted into their lives for this part of it. Perhaps along with the new or age-old vows, there should be a special blessing upon the marriage.

The following is a Blessing that my wife Mardell and I had the privilege of giving to a fine young couple during their ceremony:

"There is something about the continuity of generations that is amazing. This present generation of which, you, Jason and Temple, represent, is the culmination of many generations.

"As best as we can calculate, there are something like twenty generations of believers behind you. Like streams flowing across the land, blending and melding into each other, your grandparents, great-grandparents, and great-great-grandparents, both maternal and paternal, family after family have been faithful to God.

"This is God's plan for Jews and Gentiles alike. God promised Abraham that He would bless Isaac, and a thousand generations beyond him, if they would serve Him. It is with this same promise to all believers that we invoke God's new Covenant Blessing upon you, Jason and Temple.

"This is your personal paraphrase of Isaiah 59:21:

'As for me, this is my Covenant with the Simmons and the Hornshuhs, the Veils and the Burkes,' says the Lord. 'My Spirit, who is upon you, and my words that I have put in your mouth will not depart from your mouths, Temple and Jason, or from the mouths of your descendants from this time on and forever, says the Lord.'

"Jason and Temple, your friends are here to bless you. I have found that our friends over the years have blessed us in so many ways. While a young boy, living in a parsonage, scores of pastors, missionaries, and families came through our town and church, and stayed in our home.

"I remember one person in particular. Temple, he was your great-grandfather, Fred Hornshuh. I was a boy of about 12 years old, and I was standing in the aisle waiting for church to begin. This man came up to me and asked my name. When I told him it was Dan LeLaCheur, he said, "You must be Clarence LeLaCheur's son." I said I was, and he said, "Well, you are going into the ministry, aren't you?" What could I say? So, I said, "Yes, I guess so." He then took a dollar from his wallet, and said, "Here is the first dollar for your ministry." Then he put his hand on my head and prayed a blessing on me.

"I have never forgotten that moment and the power of his blessing on my life. I trust today that as we pray a blessing for you with your parents and these friends that this will be just such a momentous time in your lives as that moment was in mine.

> Jason and Temple, may the Lord Jesus Christ be with you from this day on. May He defend you, may He lead you, and may He protect you. Almighty God ,bless this man, Jason, and this woman, Temple, by the word of Your mouth. Unite their hearts in the enduring bond of pure love. May you be blessed by your families. May you be blessed with your children and grandchildren. May the love you lavish on them be empowered by a special anointing of the Holy Spirit. Oh God, place Your peace in their hearts and home. Give them godly friends who will stand with them in joy and in sorrow. Dear Jesus, bless them with a home that will be a haven for many. Bless them with compassion for the hurting and a love for lost souls.

"Jason and Temple, in the name of Jesus, I bless you as you follow God's calling upon your lives. I pray that the desire for earthly possessions will never lead you astray. May your hearts' focus always be upon treasures laid up for you in heaven. Now, may the blessing of a good long life be yours, and may your love grow. May the vows that you take today continue in their great legacy. It is with full faith and trust in the name of Jesus that we proclaim this blessing upon you, Jason and upon you, Temple. Amen."

5. Business

I am convinced that we can put our trust in God for this area of our lives. Being equally yoked together in this arena of life is also very important. One cannot be divided in business morals any more than in his or her marriage. Therefore, it is keenly important that the parent's blessing lead their children into their career no matter what it may be.

6. Ministry

Finding one's gift is important in all phases of life, whether as a schoolteacher, lawyer, salesperson, or missionary. Part of the long-term process of the Blessing is helping one's children learn how to accept who they are (identity), and how to walk the road of life (destiny) in an effective manner.

I heard this bit of advice years ago, and I have passed it on to dozens of young people. If you can be a businessperson, be happy, and share your faith, do not be a pastor. Go into full-time ministry only if you know that is absolutely where God wants you. I am confident God will not call you to any kind of work, secular or religious without giving you the gifts and abilities to carry it forward. This is part of a Family Blessing: the trust to be what you are called to be.

The Power of the Blessing

The Blessing is a stamp of approval on the child's future, his or her identity, destiny, and dream of the future. The Blessing becomes stronger with each generation. Most often, the next generation will turn the parents' dream into a new and larger dream.

The sad thing is that this principle also works with the Curse. It too becomes stronger with each generation, unless it is broken. The Scripture is true: the sins of the parents are visited upon the children, the grandchildren, and even to the great-grandchildren.

We know the Bible teaches that each person will be punished for his or her own sins. How then shall we interpret Numbers 14:18, which mentions "visiting the sins of the fathers upon their children to the third and fourth generation." I believe this passage refers to the fact that parents pass on to their children sinful patterns of behavior. A few examples are anger, untruthfulness, alcoholism, and beliefs. "Ahaziah did evil in the eyes of the Lord, because he walked in the ways of his father and mother...who caused Israel to sin" (1 Kings 22:52). In Jeremiah 9:14 we read of those who followed the Baals, as their father taught them. These Scriptures explain that a sinful environment or pattern of actions is passed on from one generation to the next.

Not Just A Formal Rite

The Blessing is not something old-fashioned. It is not just a Jewish tradition. Rather, it is ancient. It is eternal!

Jeremiah 6:16 states, "Thus says the Lord, 'Stand by the way and see and ask for the Ancient paths, where the good way is, and walk in it: and you will find rest for your souls.' But they said, 'We will not walk in it.'"

The Hebrew word *olam* from which we derive the word "ancient" has several meanings: Hidden, concealed, universal, perpetual, timeless, eternal, and out of eternity. I have come to realize that these ways are not just ways of men, but rather the eternal ways of God. They are universal life principles, not just applicable to the Jewish culture, or *any* specific culture, but for all mankind.

The Blessing: A Principle That Makes Life Work

The Blessing is similar to the following principles that make life function:

Belief in God—If a person doesn't believe in God, he will always be changing his focus and direction because he essentially believes only in himself, or of a more ambiguous nature, the philosophies of the world.

Faith—A dynamic faith in God is the most life-sustaining force of a person's experience.

Prayer—Prayer is more than talking, taking sacraments, or even listening. Prayer is the opening of one's mind, spirit, and body, so one not only feels God's heartbeat, but is literally fed and empowered by it until His heartbeat becomes a sustaining force.

Marriage—When God created Adam and then realized Adam was still incomplete, He created Eve, which caused Adam to say, "Wow." The "wow" of life is knowing the fruit of a commitment to your husband or wife.

Honesty—Honesty is the result of your honor, which says *who* you are, and *what* you are.

Faithfulness—Faithfulness is the tenacity to never give up. Never stop believing. Never substitute the easy way, or the selfish way, for what is right.

Sacredness of life—It is too bad we have allowed unbelievers to steal from us the ancient paths that are key to successful and prosperous families. Let us take for example the sanctity of life. How sad that we have allowed one of God's most precious gifts and dehumanized it to a mere choice. We can now morally and legally let a baby live—who is receiving life immediately after conception—or we can kill it. This wonderful gift of life has been minimized by the choice of death rather than life, because several generations have been taught that a woman's *choice* is the greatest gift they have at their disposal. The words have been clothed in ignorance; "fetus" instead of "child," and "abortion" instead of "murder."

I will always remember driving through the streets of a town in Jamaica several years ago. Since my nationality was obvious, I was berated block after block with the shouts of, "Baby killer!" It seemed like it would never end. I, a baby killer? These words describing my great homeland that I could do nothing about? Yes, I was being called a baby killer. I felt that I was literally being cursed for the sin of my country. I was made aware that generation after generation will suffer far more for this national sin than I did that day. What one generation does lives on in the lives of the next generation.

Jeremiah 6:16 tells us that when we walk in the ancient paths, we will find rest for our souls. Many people spend a lifetime trying to become valuable, because they feel valueless on the inside. They are trying to be a success, by earning enough money, degrees, high positions, or even doing a great work for God, maybe even trying to be a super mom, or super dad. None of these accomplishments is bad, in fact, they all are good, but if these people never received a blessing of love and acceptance from their parents, they may still feel empty.

I talk to believers 30, 40, 50 and years older who are still trying to figure out what they want to be when they grow up. This is not normal. It is common, but it is not normal.

They wonder: "Am I really loved?" "Am I really valuable?" "Am I doing anything that has any meaning?"

These deep questions of the soul should be settled right at the time of puberty through a powerful impartation of identity and destiny from God, coming through a father and mother. In cultures where this rite of passage is still practiced, there is very little gender confusion in adulthood. Most people experience a strong sense of belonging, value, significance, and destiny.

A Jewish man, Jeff Brodsky, said that as much as he loved his wife, and as special as his wedding day was, there is one day that stands out more in his mind than even his wedding day. That was the day of his Bar Mitzvah ceremony. He said that it was the most important day of his life.

"I can remember at what moment I woke up, because I looked at the clock. I remember what I ate for breakfast. The clothes I wore to the Synagogue, and what people said to me. It was the day I became a man!"

Once again, this is not just a Jewish tradition, but is *olam*, an ancient path meant for every son and daughter. In the Jewish culture, a son or daughter experiences this ceremony of blessing into adulthood.

In addition to the traditionally named events of Bar Mitzvah or Bat Mitzvah, some have named them, Bar Imrah (*son of promise*), or Bat Imrah, (*daughter of promise*), and Bar Simcha (*son of joy*), or Bat Simcha (*daughter of joy*). I would like to suggest that, as believers in Jesus the Messiah, we call our Blessing: Son of the New Covenant and Daughter of the New Covenant.

Part II

One of the great joys of my life is to hear how God has released His favor on families who begin to seriously practice the Blessing in their homes. It is amazing to note the positive attitude changes, character improvements, restored health, and whole families coming to salvation.

It is God's plan and intention that every son and daughter should receive a powerful impartation of Identity, Destiny, and Vision from God coming through a father and mother at the time of passing from adolescence to adulthood. It brings emotional closure to childhood and releases the son or daughter into adulthood. This is so important that Jesus Himself did not begin His ministry without first receiving this blessing from his Heavenly Father.

Preparation

The preparation preceding the ceremony is as important as the ceremony itself.

At around 11 or 12 years of age, most children are uniquely prepared by God to receive instruction regarding adulthood from their parents. Children's hearts still tend to be very open to their parents at this time in life as they are not yet consumed with as many activities as they will be in a couple of years. Most children still enjoy spending time with their parents at this age.

It is probably best to have a regular weekly meeting with your son or daughter for a six-month period or longer. It would be a good idea to make a special date alone with each parent. Various topics of manhood and womanhood should be discussed. Relationship and mentorship should be concentrated on more than content at this time. Remember, the child is being prepared to take spiritual responsibility for his or her own life. Up until this time of Blessing, the parents have been in charge of carrying this spiritual responsibility.

This time of preparation is to help prepare the child for the following six areas of life:

1. To enter into a settled and peaceful sense of adult identity
2. To enter into a clear and settled sense of destiny
3. To have an understanding of the parents' vision for his or her life
4. To be emotionally released into manhood or woman-hood at the time of the family Blessing ceremony
5. To take adult responsibility for his or her own spiritual health from the time of this Blessing
6. To walk in emotional and sexual purity all the days of his or her life

Participants

- The son or daughter who is being affirmed and blessed by parents and family
- Parents, grandparents, and any of the following: uncles, aunts, brothers, sisters, and other close family members and special friends
- Plan ahead: Make sure that the one receiving the bless-ing and the primary ones doing the blessing are placed so they can be seen, and that the microphone is portable enough so that each person speaking can be heard. When the parents or persons are placing their hands on the son or daughter, make certain that they are seen and heard.

The set-up could be something like this:

Mother   Family
            Son or Daughter
Father

Congregation & Guests

Elements of the Blessing

The Blessing is not a sermon. The Blessing is not an admonition. This is not the purpose nor the time to be teaching or correcting. It calls down God's grace upon the one being blessed. The blessing is an affirmation of *positive* characteristics. It should include at least the following five components.

1. A confirmation of gender identity
2. A release into manhood or womanhood
3. A calling forth of positive character qualities
4. A recital of any prophetic words that have been given to him or her
5. A pronouncement of specific personal blessings from the father and mother on the son or daughter

This Blessing ceremony helps to create an emotional closure to childhood and a release into adulthood. I believe this ceremony should be a big deal, making a statement to your son or daughter. It may cost something, but it will be well worth the expense. It should also contain meaningful symbols, which could be a ring, a locket, an article of clothing, a certificate, a Bible, or perhaps a family heirloom.

Primitive tribes make permanent marks on the physical body as tokens of going through this meaningful rite of passage. Perhaps much of the body piercing that takes place today among young people is a counterfeit of the legitimate need for a tangible, visible token of adulthood.

This ceremony should be so meaningful that the young life is empowered with a vision for the future. It creates a moment of transition. The ceremony conveys the message: "Your life will never be the same again. You will never be a little boy or girl again. You are entering into a new season." This happens at a Bar or Bat Mitzvah. It happens at a wedding ceremony. It happened for Jesus at the River Jordan.

There should be specific commitments made by the young person:

- I will assume responsibilities for my behavior.
- I will seek God's will for every area of my life.
- I will make other personal commitments (specified).

There should be specific commitments made by the parents:

- "I want you to know my love for you and my belief and trust in you."
- "If I have ever failed you, or hurt you in any way, I ask for your forgiveness. Please forgive me."

A Proposed Order of Service

Music: Choose a piece of music that is meaningful to the one being blessed, and/or has special meaning for other members of the family.

Prayer: This prayer can be given by someone who has had a great deal of influence upon the life of the son or daughter.

Purpose of the ceremony: This is an explanation of the event (or a sermon) by the pastor or appropriate person.

Introductions: First, the person being blessed, then parents and other member of the family and friends participating in the ceremony.

Scripture: The mother, father, grandparent or friend can read the Scripture.

There are many wonderful and appropriate Scriptures that may be read. If the family has a favorite Scripture that has spoken to them over the years, this should be included in the reading.

Appropriate Scriptures to use during the Blessing, Prayer, or a time of reading are:

> Numbers 6:23-26 (insert their names)
> Ephesians 3:14-19
> Deuteronomy 28:3-6 (you might paraphrase)
> Psalm 121:5-8
> Psalm 128 (adapt cities, etc.)
> Hebrews 13:21-22
> Psalm 20:1-2,4-5
> 2 Thessalonians 2:16-17
> Romans 15:5-6,13,33
> 2 Thessalonians 3:16
> Psalm 112:1b-4,6
> 1 Thessalonians 5:23-24,28

Letters: Read letters to the Blessing recipient from men of God or women of spiritual beauty. Parents should ask guests to attend well in advance of the Blessing date. However, letters from members of the family who find it impossible to be there are very appropriate.

Words of Blessing: The blessing by the mother and father should be well thought out, written down to be placed in a book of memories. Words of blessing from other people, like grandparents, are appropriate.

Prayer of Blessing: This should be done by at least one of the parents, plus other appropriate people.

Presentation of a significant symbol by a parent: This might be a ring, locket, Bible, or family heirloom. It is good to give them something that will kept for years or the rest of their lives. This symbol can be shown to their children in anticipation of the day they will be blessed by their parents.

Response: If planned, a response from the Blessing recipient is very good, not only for the family and guests, but for the recipient as well.

Sample Blessings and Prayers

Words of Blessing from the Father:

For example: "Josh, I am so glad that God has given you to our family. We could not have asked for a son who would be any different. Josh, if I have ever injured you or wronged you through actions or words, please forgive me. If I have not cleared up any misunderstanding, please forgive me. I am very sorry.

"You are a wonderful son. I love you very, very much, and I am so proud to be your father. Your name 'Joshua' means 'God of salvation.' What a powerful declaration!

"Josh, you are no longer a little boy. Today you become a man. God has given you a very keen mind, and the gift to articulate your ideas and plans. I believe God will enhance the gifts that you have and that you will be able to win many to Christ and to help many find the peace of knowing Him. Josh, I bless not only your abilities and gifts, I bless you with a life of sexual purity, so that you might bring to your marriage and your own children all that will help you to be a wonderful, responsible husband and father.

"Joshua, I release you to be all that God wants you to be in body, mind, and spirit. I bless you now and pray that you will fulfill your destiny in life."

Prayer of Blessing by the Mother:

For example: "Father, I thank You for our son Joshua. His father and I join in blessing him today. You have equipped

Josh with so many wonderful characteristics and gifts. We pray that he may be released completely to use them always in a positive and spiritual manner. We bless his future, the girl that You are preparing for him even now to marry, and the children they will bring into this world. Father, we bless our son who this very day we declare to be a man. Guide him in his life's work and ministry. Let each calling of his life be in Your perfect will.

"Joshua, in the name of Jesus we honor and bless you. We pray that God will carry on through you the vision of a godly family that He has blessed for generations. In the name of Jesus, we pray this blessing. Amen."

Sample Blessing from the Mother:

For example, "Rebecca, you are a bright and shining light in our family. Your father and I feel extremely blessed by God to be your parents. Becky, I remember a couple years ago, a disagreement that we had over a minor problem. Please forgive me if I was ever unthoughtful or selfish in our discussions. I want you to know that you are a God-given light in my life. Your name 'Rebecca' means 'bound.' You have always been bound to God.

"Becky, you have an ability to make people feel and act better than they ever thought they could. You bring such warmth and love into every room. You care not only for the best of people, but you have such a gift of accepting and caring for the hurting and the helpless.

"Rebecca, you are no longer a little pink-cheeked girl. From this day on you are moving into being an adult. We honor that, and declare a blessing upon your womanhood. We bless the decisions that you will be making in the future. We bless your purity, and your integrity. We know, dear daughter, that you will make good decisions about all the issues that pertain to your being a wife and a mother.

"When the words were spoken over you at your dedication: 'That you would be a person of sterling character, and guided by a mission of truth and love,' we accepted that, and prayed often that this would be fulfilled in your life. Becky, it has. We release you today to move on and fulfill all that God intends for your life. May you find peace and love. May you prosper and be the woman of God to all ages. Becky, in the name of Jesus, we bless you on this important day and for all days to come."

Prayer of Blessing by the Father:

For example: "Our loving heavenly Father, our hearts still cling to this wonderful daughter as a little girl, but our minds and spirits tell us she is now a woman of God. We pray, God, that You will keep Becky in emotional and physical health. We declare her love for You, and her desire to serve You, and her goal to reach other young people for Christ. We pray that Becky will be steadfast and kept in sexual purity. We pray a fence of protection and blessing around and over her life.

"We now release Rebecca to life as an adult, to know good friends, to have a godly and wholesome marriage, and to be blessed with a wonderful and loving family.

"Bless her, Oh God, as we lay our hands of love upon her today. Jesus, we pray that Becky may know health, spiritually and physically. We bestow upon her today a destiny and vision of truth and power.

"In the name of Jesus, we release you, Rebecca, to run the race of life with our love and prayers, and the power of the Holy Spirit to guide you. Amen."

Finally

There is no right way to do anything that we have talked about in this parental blessing. The perfect way is to just do it! Keep the ceremony filled with love and respect.

Forgive where needed, and let that son or daughter know how you will always be proud of them. The results of this action will bring a change in your legacy for many generations. I have had countless pastors tell me that this is the most exciting and important service of the year in their church.

Celebration

The Family Blessing leads to celebration just like a wedding reception where you serve food, toast to the couple, sing, talk, and remember. Whatever you do, design this event to be appropriate for the occasion. You will want to hold it in the church's fellowship hall where the celebration's nature can be less formal. In the Jewish culture, the young person sits in a chair while the men of the community lift him in the chair on their shoulders and dance with him around the reception hall.

Following the time of eating and celebration you may wish to open the microphone to allow further blessings by family and friends. You may ask in advance for certain people to participate with things that would be appropriate, such as a Scripture verse, a prophetic word, a poem written in his or her honor, a special song, or a positive story recounting his or her godly character.

Please do not recount stories or words that would embarrass, belittle, or shame the moment. We are launching this person into a very serious and meaningful time of life. Have a great time, but honor this one and glorify God.

A Family-Only Blessing

This same blessing can also be given in a more private setting. We did this with each of our four grandsons. Most of the time, they lived in one part of the country and we another. When we would visit them, we would gather as many relatives as possible. It would be "Ryan's Day," for example. We would have a family meal that Ryan had chosen. Then at the close of the meal we would read a Scripture verse and explain the significance. We then would go around the table while all members of the family gave their blessing of love and anticipation. Then the parents gave their blessing, after which we would all gather around the young man and pray. Yes, it was a powerful and meaningful time in each of their lives. I would urge you to consider this method if you cannot do a public service where all their family, friends and peers can be present.

At our family-only Blessing events, we would take a picture during the prayer with each of the grandsons. We would then make a plaque with the picture, date, place, a Scripture, and the meaning of their name on it. This plaque, along with a Bible signed by all the family members, would be presented to the Blessing recipient.

The following pictures, plaques, certificates and letters are just a few of the ways in which this Family Blessing can become more meaningful.

Thanks to those who so willingly let us use their personal ideas of making their blessings meaningful.

You may wish to use these as springboards for ideas to make a blessing come alive in your own family.

Pastor Tom and Nancy Rupli, their son Josh and his wife Victoria, blessing their unborn baby, James, who is now three months old.

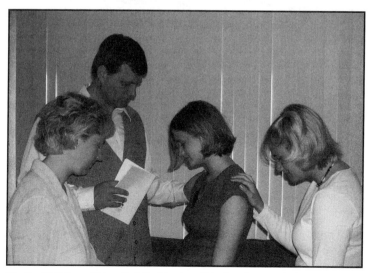

Dr. David Cole and his wife Julie, blessing Abigail and Hannah their daughters

We gave these four plaques to our four grandsons following their blessings.

Nathan Lee Smith

"A Gift Given by God"

Born
June 3, 1987

Family Blessing
July 4, 2002

"The steps of a good man are ordered by the Lord"
Psalm 37:23

BRANDON JONATHAN SMITH

"Man of Victory"

Born
March 16, 1983

Family Blessing
December 28, 1996

*"I WILL STRENGTHEN AND UPHOLD YOU WITH MY
RIGHTEOUS RIGHT HAND."
ISAIAH 41:10*

JORDAN DAVID LeLaCHEUR REMUS

"Man of God"

Born
April 24, 1984

Family Blessing
April 25, 1999

"YOU WILL SOAR ON WINGS LIKE EAGLES"
ISAIAH 40:31

RYAN DANIEL SMITH

"Man of Distinction"

Born
December 17, 1979

Family Blessing
October 10, 1994

*"MY SPIRIT WILL NOT DEPART FROM YOU
OR FROM YOUR CHILDREN"
ISAIAH 59:21*

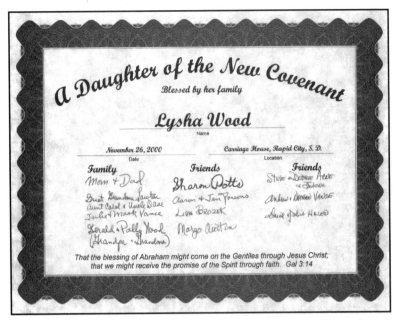

A Daughter of the New Covenant

Blessed by her family

Lysha Wood
Name

November 26, 2000 — Date

Carriage House, Rapid City, S. D. — Location

Family	Friends	Friends
Mom + Dad	Sharon Potts	Steve & Debbie Atwe of Selcise
Great Grandma Lawton	Aaron + Jen Parsons	Andrew & Nathan Vance
Aunt Carol & Uncle Dave	Lisa Brozek	David & Julie Haver
Julie + Mark Vance	Margo Austin	
Gerald & Polly Wood (Grandpa + Grandma)		

That the blessing of Abraham might come on the Gentiles through Jesus Christ;
that we might receive the promise of the Spirit through faith. Gal 3:14

This is a sample certificate that we have used for those who have been blessed.

Chris Meisner being lifted in the "Bar Mitzvah Chair" by his friends and parents Bob and Audrey Meisner of Winnipeg, Manitoba, Canada, during his Christian Blessing.

Blessings

The sixth grade blessing provided us with a real intentional way of communicating our blessings to our daughter. The entire process, including the classes Chelsea attended, the letters her relatives wrote, creating her display, and preparing for the celebration, gave new meaning to the time when our daughter would pass from childhood into young adulthood. We look back on the blessing as a significant moment in her life.

Judy and Kelly Kight, Spokane, Washington
Parents of Chelsea a sixth grader who was blessed

To Chelsea: I am glad that we can take time, as a family, to let you know how much we love you. I appreciate your kindhearted nature. I know you genuinely care for the people around you and are a faithful friend. Your mom and I are truly blessed to have a daughter like you. Not only do we love you, but we like you as well. You are fun to be around.

Love, Dad

The sixth grade blessing was a time of affirming our girls, Kelsey and Keri and giving them something to remember of the occasion. Gwyn and I had an opportunity to visit the Holy Land and we purchased rings in Bethlehem for each of their 6th grade blessing. The rings are different and special for each child. It is a symbol of commitment, of us as their parents that we value, support, and love them; and to our children to remain pure and true to their values.

Scot and Gwyn Burden, Spokane, Washington

Mark and Paula Sterns of Dallas, Texas have done a wonderful job of blessing their two sons. Here are a few of the steps they took.

Letter Sent to Family and Friends of Matthew Sterns

Dear Family and Friends of Matthew:

Today, April 17, 1996, Matthew Christian Sterns turned 12 years old. We are writing to you because you have been significant in Matthew's life in one way or another. You have gifts or character qualities that Paula and I have admired and desire a transfer of that blessing to Matthew.

Matthew means "gift of God" and Christian means "belonging to Christ." Matthew is a gift of God to us and we have dedicated him to Jesus Christ, not only at birth but we continue to do so now. He was the child for whom we longed and prayed.

Over this next year, would you consider input into Matthew's life? It could be any number of things: teaching him about a practical area where you are skilled; sharing a life lesson with him, whether a mistake or a triumph; instructing him in a character trait you have learned or acquired; explaining one of the fruits of the Spirit where the Lord has given you grace; encouraging him, praying for him; observing him and offering counsel or direction.

How you do this is up to you. It could be a phone call, a personal conversation, or letter; it could be a one-time brief moment of sharing or a giving of yourself over a period of time.

When Matthew turns 13, we plan on honoring his entry toward manhood by celebrating a Christ-centered bar mitzvah. Your participation in any form this year would be appreciated.

Mark and Paula Sterns, Dallas, Texas

Mark and I decided to call his Bar Mitzvah, Bar Imrah, meaning "A Son of Promise." We contacted our friend Clarence Wagner, in Jerusalem and he helped us with the procedures, purpose and times for his Bar Mitzah. Matthew told us ahead of time that he would be giving a response to becoming a man, being declared a man, and being blessed in his manhood and it was priceless.

Paula Sterns

Dear Matthew:

Today is the day when you enter manhood in the eyes of God, your family and your friends. While I have not been physically there for you this year…I have been praying for you. I remember our time together in Dallas the afternoon I gave you your journal with some prayerful insights I had for you…

As you step into manhood today, I want to remind you of some of these insights. [This is just the outline of the wonderful message Clarence gave to Matthew.]

1. Trust in the Lord
2. Laugh at yourself
3. Honor your father and mother
4. Look for the best in others
5. God is always there

6. Leave a legacy

God bless you, Matthew. This is the first day of an exciting adventure with God as He guides your steps into the special calling He has for you.

Clarence Wagner
Bridges for Peace
Jerusalem

From the program of Matthew's Bar Imrah:

MATTHEW STERNS
"A SON OF PROMISE"

Music Prelude
(Matt's Favoites)

The Commission
Glen Terrell (Pastor, Grace Vineyard)
"Man After God's Own Heart"

The Mentor
Randy Hylton (Co-pastor, Grace Vineyard)

The Heritage
Rev. Verl Sterns, Manley McGregor
Matthew's Grandfathers

The Blessing
The Elders of Grace Vineyard and Relatives
"A Man You Would Write About"

The Response
Matthew Sterns

The Benediction

Following the Benediction you are invited to a
Celebration in the Fellowship Room
Thanks for blessing Matthew!

TYLER JOEL STERNS
BAR SIMCHA
"A Son of Joy"

Again, we wrote to godly men that we wanted to mentor Tyler. The list was different, as his interests and teachers were different.

A highlight for Tyler was a friend that had come into his life 2 years earlier—A.C. Greene of the Dallas Mavericks. Tyler had won an essay contest and he got to fly with the team to a game in Phoenix, Arizona and stay in the same hotel. The highlight was spending time with his hero, A.C. Greene and playing basketball with him. They still keep in touch and he is a hero and a man of God.

Tyler gave a response to the celebration and it was great! (He didn't let us read it ahead of time, so we were floored by his young wisdom...)

Invitation to Chad David Trentham's Blessing:

ROYAL PROCLAMATION

Be it Known to All Men

WHEREAS Sir Chadwick David Trentham completed Franklin Piece High School, and Graduates on June 12, 2003.

WHEREAS he served as Jr. Class President, and

WHEREAS he served as Vice President of the Student Body his Senior year, and

WHEREAS he will graduate with honors, and

WHEREAS he has completed seven years of playing his trombone, and

WHEREAS he loves the Lord Jesus with all his heart, and

WHEREAS his mother and father are very proud of him.

BE IT PROCLAIMED, that the day of Saturday, June 14th be set aside to celebrate his graduation, and

BE IT PROCLAIMED, that at 3:00PM there will be **"The Passing of the Blessing"** Ceremony bestowed upon him by his parents.

BE IT PROCLAIMED, that honored guests will be Pastor Ole Hansen who dedicated him, Mary Jane Sanford who made his first tux, honored Sunday School teachers, children and youth pastors.

I affix my seal to this Proclamation on June 14 in the year of our Lord MMIII
Sir Douglas Trentham, father
First Lady Wilda Trentham, mother

ৡ IX ৢ

What Moms and Dads Give Their Families

Part I

What Mother's Give Their Children

One of the most beautiful and peaceful pictures is that of a mother holding her child. It brings a sense of peace and tranquility to viewers. Memories flood their mind as they remember the times they held their child or grandchild in much the same way. God has put within women the desire and wonderful ability to be the nurturer of their children. Often times we even see women being very effective nurturers to children not their own.

Note: Mardell LeLaCheur who has served in the ministry with Dan for the past 50 years writes Part I of this chapter. She taught at Open Bible College in Des Moines, Iowa for several years. She now serves her denomination as director of Women's Ministries. She and Dan have worked as a team in conducting Family Seminars all across America. While pastoring in Des Moines, Iowa, they hosted a talk radio program and a television program, both called Family Survival. Mardell has been an integral part of the LeLaCheur ministry.

Looking at the Scriptures, we see two accounts of the influence of mothers on their children. We are familiar with 2 Timothy 1:5, which states, "I have been reminded of your sincere faith, which first lived in your grandmother Lois and in your mother Eunice and, I am persuaded, now lives in you also."

What a strong statement from Paul to Timothy that the importance of his heritage is what will continue with him in his ministry. We too are admonished to pass on this wonderful faith to our children and grandchildren.

On the other hand, we read in Ezekiel 16:44, "Everyone who quotes proverbs will quote this proverb about you: 'Like mother, like daughter.' This is not a compliment to Judah. Rather it is a foretelling of doom. They will be passing down the same idolatry and judgment as an evil mother might pass on to her daughter, one of the closest and most binding curses of any relationship.

We know that when God creates something beautiful, such as the relationship of mother and child, Satan will often take that relationship and tarnish it with sin and evil, which will be passed from generation to generation.

There is a concept called "Role Theory," which delineates the influence of parents upon their children. Below is a brief outline of that concept.

Fathers are a:
- Husband to daughter
- Teacher to son

Mothers have:
- Greatest influence on moral judgment for children

Father develops sexual identity for both boys and girls. Boys with dominant fathers are:
- Better adjusted

- Leaders in college
- More easily able to make decisions

Boys with dominant mothers are:
- Weak in their masculinity
- Unable to make decisions easily
- More dependent and less aggressive

Girls with dominant fathers are:
- More feminine
- Better adjusted to the opposite sex

Girls with dominant mothers are:
- More likely to define their identity by their mother

Girls with an absent father by divorce are:
- More open, sprawling, seeking more attention and praise
- More likely to spend time at places where men gather
- More frequent daters

Girls with an absent father by death are:
- Much more reserved toward men

Findings:

A father's role is more obvious, whether good or bad, while a mother's role looks more passive but carries the greater moral strength. One can see that there is a definite role played by both parents in influencing their children and grandchildren.

Influence of Godly Mothers

Another often-quoted Scripture concerning women is Proverbs 31, which includes many characteristics of the ideal woman, or "Proverbs 31 woman." Note that the first verse of Proverbs 31 states that, "These are the wise sayings of King Lemuel of Massa, taught to him at his mother's knee" (The Living Bible).

We are teaching our children at all times. Memories of my mother are of her singing songs to me and telling me stories of her coming from Iowa to Utah and then on to Washington State, or about the times she swam in the irrigation ditches when it was so warm in Utah. When did I hear these stories? While she was sitting at the sewing machine making clothes for me. Was that planned by my mother? I doubt it, but those stories, and the memories of her telling them, are with me even today. We are teaching principles and telling stories at every opportunity in our daily lives. There isn't a "right" or best time to share your life and impart principles of good and holy living. The time to share is when one goes for a walk, rides in the car, cooks, does housekeeping, teaches skills in the home, or just has fun shopping.

Dr. Phil, on his television show, explained the influence that parents have on their children. He so casually stated the deep truth: "We learn what we live." What are we living in our homes? Are we living with yelling, sarcasm, bullying and disrespect? Or are we hearing the stories of when you were a little girl, and the stories of your spiritual walk with the Lord? These activities model to your children how they should live. Mothers and daughters have in common their understanding of aging. It is great to be able to reflect with our children and grandchildren how we felt about aging when we were young. Here is a revealing look at our view of aging.

Aging Is a Funny Thing

Do you realize that the only time in our lives when we like to get old is when we're kids?

If you're less than 10 years old, you're so excited about aging that you think in fractions.

How old are you? "I'm four and a half." You're never 36 and a half, but you're four and a half going on five. That's the key.

You get into your teens, now they can't hold you back. You jump to the next number. How old are you? "I'm gonna be 16." You could be 12, but you're gonna be 16. And then the greatest day of your life happens, you become 21. Even the words sound like a ceremony, you "become" 21. Yes! But, then you turn 30. Ooh, what happened there? Makes you sound like bad milk: "He turned so we had to throw him out." There's no fun now. What's wrong? What changed?

You "become" 21, you "turn" 30, then, you're "pushing" 40. Stay over there, it's all slipping away. Then you reach 50 and "make it" to 60. You didn't think you'd make it! But you've built up so much speed that you hit 70. And after that, it's a day-by-day thing. From there you hit Wednesday, then Thursday, then Friday. You get into your 80s, you hit lunchtime, then 4:30, then 5:30, then bedtime. My grandmother won't even buy green bananas. (It's an investment you know and maybe a bad one.) It doesn't end there. Into the 90s you start going backward. I was "just" 92. Finally, a strange thing happens: If you make it over 100, you become a kid again and say, "I'm 100 and a half"

Author unknown

Influence of a Godly Grandmother

I can't mention the positive influence mothers have without relating what a double influence grandmothers have on their grandchildren. Grandmothers have that special relationship with their grandchildren that gives the grandchild support and a buffer against the world and even a place to escape from their parents.

What beautiful memories some of us have of a godly grandmother. I was allowed to have total run of my grandmother's kitchen. What a learning experience and what a trusted feeling I had to know my grandmother would allow me to sift the flour in her big flour bin and help her with the baking of bread and sugar cookies. She was my comfort and protector against the world.

I remember the time I was with my grandson, Jordan, at a Kidsports (community league) basketball game. It so happened that his parents and Papa couldn't attend that game. Jordan was in the third grade and was not the biggest kid on either team, but to me he was the best. The opposing team had boys who must have been 12 years of age—anyway they *looked* the size of 12-year-olds and they played a rough-and-ready game of basketball.

Several of the boys on Jordan's team had been hit hard enough to fall to the floor, but when Jordan was hit so hard that he fell crying and holding his leg, I was beside myself. It felt as though he had been on the floor two or three minutes, with nobody appearing to help him, ask him if he could walk, or anything. So I marched out to the little guy in the middle of the floor to ask if his leg was hurting too badly to stand. About that time the much-too-young referee walked up to me and said, "You can't be out here on this floor."

I stood up pointed my finger at him and said, "Don't tell me what to do, I'm his *grandmother*." Well, that obviously wasn't good enough as he had authority: With one point of *his* finger he said "I'm kicking you out of this gym."

I had to leave, but as I walked the limping Jordan back to the bench, he looked up at me and said, "Mimi, I'm so glad you are here."

Did it matter that I was kicked out of that game? Not on your life; I was Jordan's protector and he needed me at that moment. I became the mother bear with her cub at that moment, and nothing was going to stop me from protecting him.

That is part of being a mother and grandmother. We are born with that innate power of protection and nurturing, and when it is done in a positive way, it is the greatest influence of their moral judgment later on in life.

Influence of an Ungodly Mother

The most powerful role model for a child is the same-sex parent. This may be why Ezekiel warned Judah that they would do evil just as the influence of an evil mother influences her daughter to be just like her. Ezekiel 16:44 states, "Everyone who quotes proverbs will quote this proverb about you: 'Like mother, like daughter.'"

When a mother uses her tongue to lash out against her daughter, diminishing her personhood, it will only continue from generation to generation. This child becomes what she is told, which might be: No good, ugly, dumb, sloppy, lazy, fat. These words will live on in the memory of our children's minds for their entire life. Just as the memories of wonderful moments stay with us, the negative words become who we are and they often overshadow the good things that were done in our childhood.

A young woman came to Dan out of desperation. She was tormented by an incident in her life that still troubled her in her adult years. She was told when she was a child that if she misbehaved, her mother was going to put her in an institution. This wasn't a one-time warning, it became a repeatedly-used tool of discipline. One day when she had been especially bad, she feared that this would be it—she would be sent to the institution. That night she took her pillowcase from her bed and stuffed her Barbie doll and a few favorite toys in it so she could carry it with her to the institution.

Why would a grown woman remember and relate that pitiful story to Dan? Because it had left a negative mark in her life, and she knew she had to forgive to be released from this threat, so she would not pass it on to her children.

We are on a beautiful journey of life and have the most wonderful opportunity to bless our children and grandchildren and the children that come into our lives. The positive and uplifting words that we speak to children will live with them long after we are gone. Proverbs 12:6 states, "The words of the wicked kill; the speech of the upright saves" (THE MESSAGE).

We can make great memories for them. We can speak positive words into their lives that will build their confidence. We can pray over them and they will know the power of that prayer. We can sing praises to them as they grow spiritually.

A good example of a mother's impact is a statement made by Bern Williams, "Sooner or later we all quote our mothers."

Part II

What Fathers Give Their Children

Children crave the presence of a father, yet today nearly 50 percent of children grow up without a father.

Some men don't know how to be a father, however. Men don't have to be perfect, men don't even have to have an exact plan for their fathering skills. They simply need to be engaged in their son's and daughter's lives.

The ABCs of Father-Child Goals

Fathers can help their children in many areas of growth:

1. Acceptance of themselves

Malcolm Muggeridge, while narrating a television documentary about a community of caring for handicapped adults, heard a most memorable prayer by a handicapped adult, who had known a lifetime of personal rejection.

"God who made me as I am, help me accept myself as I am."

Undoubtedly, this is a prayer that we need to help all our children learn to pray. The basis for self-acceptance of who we are, is first of all, the acceptance of who we are by our parents.

I have never forgotten the words of a parent that were spoken in front of their six-year-old daughter, "We wanted a boy, we prayed for a boy, but I guess God did not hear our prayers and we got a girl." I still hurt when I think of that little gal hearing those words in her head until she dies.

We can start loving and accepting each baby by saying in his or her newborn presence: "What a gift! What a beautiful person you are." Or, "Your mother and I are so glad that God let you be born in our family. You are exactly what we wanted. God made you special just for us." Or, "We named you Joyce, because it means Joyful One, and you are your mother's and my joy. Oh, what joy you bring to our lives."

Continue to utter these confirmations of value at every age. There is nothing like the spoken blessing. A big part of the blessing is the child knowing and hearing your unqualified acceptance of who he or she is.

2. Bonding

Make this commitment: "I will be as close to my son, or daughter, as a parent can possibly be. My child will know me just like I longed to know my father." When you as a parent give yourself to your child, he or she will begin to understand you, with your love and caring heart, but also with your imperfections. She will notice when you make mistakes, and she will also notice when you say, "I'm sorry."

This means you must spend time with your child. You will have to talk, really talk, open up, and express your opinions. It will help you begin to verbalize opinions, feelings, joys, sorrows, and deep spiritual feelings about eternal values.

What is the advantage of bonding to your sons and daughters? You won't lose them to the world, ungodly friends, and a cult of ungodliness. Many fathers do not have the slightest idea of the power and influence they can have upon their children. You have the God-given opportunity to bring out the masculinity in your sons, and the femininity in your daughters. If you don't do it, it won't be long until some young person will get close, physically close to your child. Hugging, talking and laughing will be so pleasurable that their sexuality will come out and they will do things for which they will be sorry. You must talk—not preach—to them, loving, laughing, encouraging, sharing your feelings and beliefs. For far too long mothers have bonded, and fathers have missed their greatest opportunities of influence and love in their children's lives. Malachi 4:6 states, "He will turn the hearts of the fathers to their children, and the hearts of the children to their fathers; or else I will come and strike the land with a curse."

3. Control

Children are born without control over most bodily functions and urges that they may have. We potty train them so that eventually they get rid of diapers. We teach them how to eat, so that eventually they stop getting food all over themselves and the floor all around them.

It is sad to see a six-year-old still behaving like a one-year-old. Worse yet is to see a 25-year-old still thinking and responding to urges and stimuli like a six-year-old.

Children must be taught, modeled, and encouraged to develop self-control. Children who are kept within the bounds of certain restrictions and guidelines are happier than those without restrictions. They will test those boundaries repeatedly, but they will feel more secure and more loved when there is discipline. Discipline should not be just authoritarian all of the time. It must be handled with real love and understanding. Punishment should never be given in anger or frustration. Without a doubt, children will model their self-control after yours.

4. Discovering gifts, strengths and weaknesses

Do you know what your son's or daughter's God-given gifts are? Do you know the one thing in life that they naturally are the very best at doing? Do you know what they like to do best? Did anyone ever recognize your talents or gifts when you were a child? Did your parents help you develop them? If not, can you imagine how you could have been different if they had directed you, and encouraged you in developing your talents and gifts?

Your children's strengths, weaknesses, gifts, and talents may be very different from yours. Fathers and mothers can do their sons and daughters a lifelong favor by recognizing what God has already put in them, and helping them develop these natural God given graces.

Dads, you can be a tremendous guide to your children. When you notice their natural gifts, encourage them in those areas of life and help to develop them. Their gifts may be in athletics, music, drama, relationships, or intelligence. They may have a tremendous gift of encouragement. Help them in the areas you can see that they excel.

Spiritual gifts work in a similar way. One way of verifying a spiritual gift is determining if it is working well in the church body. If it is not, most likely they don't have the gift.

If so, encourage your son or daughter to allow that gift to prevail in his or her life.

A joke in my family is that I was going to learn to play the violin. My granddad was an old-time fiddler. He played for barn and square dances, and did it all by ear. I doubt that Granddad ever had a violin lesson in his life. He did have a very nice instrument and I remember as a boy being awed when he played the fiddle. He carved the violin tailpiece out of bone, giving the instrument a look of distinction.

When Granddad was past the fiddle-playing age, he said that whichever grandchild learned to play the violin first would have his instrument. I talked my dad into buying me a cheap little violin, so I could take lessons at school.

It wasn't that I didn't like the violin, but I just didn't have the ear for music, and my fingers were made for throwing a football not fingering the notes.

I could never be a great musician, but God gave me other gifts. I think my family also recognized before too long that music was not my cup of tea, and that my hands and fingers were not for playing the violin.

I remember them encouraging me to trust God and use my gifts of faith, mercy, and spiritual discernment. I soon learned that much like my parents, my hands were made to bless people and trust God for healing, peace, and salvation in their lives.

5. Enjoyment

Think of what is missed when a father has a distant relationship with his child. I have heard many young men say, "I am going to be the father I wanted as a child." Dads have so much to do with how the family enjoys one another, especially the one-on-one communication with each member of the family.

When I speak to men's groups, I frequently ask the question, "What is the one thing you wished you would have received more from your father? Here are the answers I always receive: 1) More time spent with me, 2) More conversation and talk, or 3) Verbal expression of love.

Some of us were fortunate enough to have terrific dads that talked with us, played with us, prayed with us, put arms around us, took us hunting and fishing, and came to ball games. However, many of us grew up with a father who never got involved. He treated his children as his own father treated him.

While you are helping bring all these things out in your children, don't let the seriousness of the task keep you from enjoying being a father and watching those little sons and daughters grow up to be exciting teens, wonderful adults, and parents to your grandchildren. Teach, model, and create enjoyment in family relationships. Many fathers grew up with the old idea that life was serious, overemphasizing discipline, and discouraging true family camaraderie.

Real love and real life should be enjoyable. Dad, you are the leader, let it happen.

6. Family traditions

Isaiah 44:3-5 states a tremendous unconditional promise for the family, "I will pour my spirit on your descendants, and my blessing on your offspring."

Every family needs to claim that. Some traditions are being ignored or forgotten. Perhaps many should be lost, but families are God-ordained and parents are to pass on a blessing like their family histories and other traditions.

In our family, we have specific times for annual celebrations, holidays, and times of blessing. These are the times for memories and making memories, for telling one another how much we love them, and for praising and worshipping God together.

7. Giving

There is a difference between genuinely giving a gift and "buying" favor or recognition. Many individuals have had a person give them something, knowing there were strings attached—maybe a physical return of some kind, or perhaps public acknowledgment. Giving should not reckless or foolish. Giving should never bring despair or heartache to either the giver or the receiver.

We can give to our children gifts that have no strings attached with no qualifications to be met. Modeling this kind of giving lifestyle is so important. By doing the act of giving, you teach your children to give. Someone may say, "Dan, don't you think honesty would be a better subject to teach our children?" But genuine giving *is* honesty.

In another area of giving, there is something to be said about teaching your children how to work hard, so they can earn more or get a better job. My brother and sisters can verify that we were instructed to work hard. No one grew up in the Clarence LeLaCheur family without learning the value of work. Dad was planting a church, raising five children and trying to make ends meet. When he came home and said to my brother or sister, "Tomorrow you start detasseling corn, we leave at 6 in the morning," we would gear up to work hard. I never regretted those jobs. They allowed me to minister in all kinds of places, both as a young boy and as an ordained minister.

Other kinds of giving:

1. A kind word or compliment
2. A pat on the back (A touch is worth a thousand words.)
3. A letter of openness and honesty
4. A lunch or a dinner alone with that son of daughter
5. An open-door policy into your life during times of hardship or victory

6. Sharing moments of your own childhood from the age your child is now
7. Passing on an heirloom that meant a lot to you
8. Being consistent with your core values despite the circumstances

A Texan made this statement: "Nothing makes the crop grow like the shadow of its owner."

This says it just as well: "Nothing makes children grow like the shadow of their father."

Review and Study Guide

After All Is Said and Done, What Are You Going To Do About It?

Today, when someone has an ailment or pain he or she will often reach for a pill. Sometimes the pill helps; sometimes it is just a temporary stopgap.

I listened to a doctor discuss this subject. He explained that many times a particular medication is hailed as a cure-all. However, before long, statistics show that not only is this new medication not working, but those taking the medication are contracting the disease at a higher rate than those who don't.

The second point this doctor made, which might explain the above phenomenon, is that individuals who receive medication to slow down or reverse a disease often choose not to give up the things that originally *caused* the disease.

The various suggestions, Scriptures, actions and prayers in this book are not to be treated like a drug. They can't fix problems by themselves. You must *act* with the understanding these words have given you.

My goal for each reader is that you absorb the truths of Scripture and apply them as suggested, opening up your heart with a prayer of faith and acceptance of God's way of life for the family.

The end of this book brings the beginning for you to take steps to transform your past and present actions into a God-given direction for the next generation to travel.

Review and Questions for Chapter I

Is it possible that you or another authority figure in your home has written graffiti on your child's life? This not-too-subtle method of undermining his or her confidence in themselves or God can lead to a very significant wound in their spirit.

What can you do?

1. Have a sincere and loving talk with this child no matter what age he or she is.
2. Admit the mistakes of placing this burden upon the son or daughter.
3. Ask for forgiveness.
4. Express your love.
5. Talk to other members of the family who may be involved in unkind or deprecating words or actions to this person.
6. Speak positively and kindly to this person.

Discussion Questions for Chapter I:

1. What are some forms of graffiti you have observed?
2. How has it affected the one(s) involved?
3. How can it be removed from this person's life?

Review and Questions for Chapter II

What is the Father Wound? Proverb 18:14 describes the depth to which the Father Wound can hurts: "A man's spirit will endure sickness, but a broken spirit who can bear?" For the man or woman who has been wounded by their father or mother, there are always severe repercussions.

Discussion Questions for Chapter II:

1. Take a moment to list any parental actions that you consider wounds in your spirit or mind. Examples could be: cruel words, rejection, and misunderstanding.

2. How have these wounds affected you?
3. Have you treated your children as you were treated as a child?

Review and Questions for Chapter III

Sexual abuse is much more prevalent than we like to imagine. Often it comes into a child's life through a family member. It is more likely that the abused child will become an offender.

In exploring physical abuse, we need to be aware that true and loving discipline is not abuse. Physical abuse is not discipline. If any of your children have been abused in this manner, it is time to take redemptive action.

Until recently, spiritual abuse was called fanaticism, characterizing an "out of focus" believer. Often this spiritual abuse was done by good but misguided individuals who thought that spiritualizing discipline would give them more power in their efforts.

I am convinced, by literally scores of people with whom I have talked and prayed, that these negative factors of life, these painful events of childhood can be removed. I have seen many wounded and abused people find healing. Here are some suggested steps to healing:

1. Refer to your list from chapter 2 of deep-seated names and events of your life.
2. Take each event one at a time. Specifically identify the event(s) and person(s) involved.
3. Ask God for forgiveness if this caused you to sin in any way.
4. Ask God to forgive the sin of the person through whom this wound came. This will help you to cut free from their hold on your life.
5. Forgive this person. As you forgive them you are for-given and released from the memories. The forgiveness,

resentment, and the other effects from years of unfor-giveness. Matthew 6:14 states, "For if you forgive men when they sin against you, your heavenly Father will also forgive you. But if you do not forgive men their sins, your Father will not forgive you."

6. Reread Chapter IV.
7. Build a hedge around your life and family. (See Hosea 2:6-7 and Job 1:9.)
8. Build an altar. Make this date special.
9. Share your experience with someone. Let them know what has happened in your life.
10. Continue to pray for this person who wounded you. Don't resent or hate. Remember, when you feel unfor-given, you tend to be unforgiving. Pray for their success, family, health, and for love, peace and forgiveness in their life.[1]

Review and Questions for Chapter IV

Anger and resentment is the result of unforgiveness. God's forgiveness is the only remedy for our healing. Our forgiveness for others sets us free from the anger and resent-ment that traps us. Forgiveness is key.

Discussion Questions for Chapter IV:
1. What makes forgiveness so powerful?
2. Does forgiveness mean you must accept what was done to you?
3. Does forgiveness mean that you forget the deed?
4. What should you do when the act of forgiving another person is rejected?

Review and Questions for Chapter V

Identity is crucial to a well-adjusted, confident, loving, expressive father and mother. We must consider what we intentionally give to our children. Parents, carefully phrase your words as you help develop a positive, productive and purposeful identity in them.

We so often compliment their appearance rather than their character. Consider using words that build: "Son, or daughter, you can do it," or, "You have such a great attitude," or "People listen to your ideas when you speak," or "I can always count on your honesty."

Pick out their traits and gifts, and build them into a positive life identity. Even in jest, you can cause a child to stop trying, to doubt his or her ability, or be uncertain as to who they are. Please do not take their formative years lightly. Their identity is so important and sometimes very fragile in these years.

Ponder Psalms 139:13-16:

For you created my inmost being;
You knit me together in my mother's womb.
I praise you because I am fearfully and wonderfully
made;
your works are wonderful, I know that full well.
My frame was not hidden from you when I was made
in the secret place.
When I was woven together in the depths of the earth,
your eyes saw my unformed body.
All the days ordained for me were written in your book,
before one of them came to be.

This speaks of God's hand upon David's unborn identity. God knew him and had created and prepared him for the awesome moment of birth. That event put that baby directly into the hands of a mother and father, who by their words and actions, continued to form the identity that God began. What an awesome privilege and opportunity!

Discussion Questions for Chapter V:

1. How would you describe to another person the identity we help develop in our children?
2. Can you describe someone you know who has a self-identity problem?
3. Can you describe how you would help a young person develop a good identity?

Review and Questions for Chapter VI

Perhaps the best way parents can help their children get on the right road to destiny is to walk that road themselves. Do not hesitate to talk about the decisions you are making concerning a job, a move, a ministry. Don't hesitate to include your family in the prayers, the plans, and the possibilities. This lets them know how to accomplish the same feats in the future. When they face the same decisions, they won't be set back with uncertainty of the decision-making process, the potholes, the hills to climb, and the victories enjoyed.

How are you shaping your sons' and daughters' destinies? Is life all fun and games, sports and beauty contests? They must learn how to handle a losing season, or a contest of unfavorable results. But make sure they know that the *result* of each contest is not their destiny, rather it is the *travel* to the results that is their destiny.

Give the following points some serious thought:

1. Prepare your children by giving them the building blocks of good judgment, trust, and discernment.
2. Teach them that prayer, thanksgiving, and praise are things to turn to in times of need or uncertainty.
3. Build into them the truths of righteousness: "The steps of a righteous man are ordered of the Lord."

4. Teach them to recognize and exhibit the fruits of the Spirit. They are great criteria for getting on the road of destiny and avoiding many of the potholes.
5. Reread the questions at the end of Chapter VI.

Review and Questions for Chapter VII

Help your sons and daughters develop a vision. One way to do this is to help them develop a mission statement. How?

1. Start early. Have them write down what they would like to do. In the short-term, medium-term, and long-term. Make it very simple. Have fun and talk about it. Don't belittle them, be positive.
2. Make this practice a little more sophisticated as your children get older. I believe by the time they are in their mid-teens, you will see these young people setting goals, dreaming larger dreams, and working to see their dreams come to fruition.
3. Keep this idea and exercise it from a realistic yet biblical perspective. You may find a different Scripture to use as a motto each year.

Here are some possible Scriptures to utilize in developing vision:

Habakkuk 2:2-3	Matthew 6:33
John 20:29	Proverbs 29:1
Philippians 3:14	2 Corinthians 4:18
Deuteronomy 6:6-9	1 Corinthians 9:24
Ephesians 1:18	Habakkuk 3:19
Hebrews 11:1	1 Peter 2:9

Review and Questions for Chapter VIII

The Family Blessing should begin at conception, but at around 13 years of age, there is a need for approval, acceptance, and a definite word of direction.

If you have never blessed your children as described in this chapter, it is not too late. If they are close to 13, plan now to make it a big deal in their lives. Even if they are 20, 30 or 40 years old, you can still do a wonderful act for them that will bless them and their generations forever.

Please do not miss this blessing for your children. You can have a public service, or a private service. The importance is in the sincerity of those involved, such as other children, parents and family members.

The included samples of blessing events, certificates, and invitations in this book are only ideas. You may develop something that is uniquely yours and wonderful for your family. Make it the biggest thing that has ever happened in your child's life.

Review and Questions for Chapter IX

Considering everything parents can give to their children. The greatest gift is a gift that commences a perpetual movement of blessing that can go on for generations.

Mother, add to your list of gifts you can give. Ask:

1. What am I giving?
2. What can I give that I have not been giving?

Fathers do the same:

1. Where am I doing a good job?
2. Where am I coming up short?

Promote blessing. Leave a legacy. Give your children the opportunity to experience life as God would have them live it.

Notes

Chapter one
1. Craig Hill, *The Ancient Paths* (Family Foundations).
2. Ibid.
3. Ibid.

Chapter two
1. Gordon Dalbey, *Father and Son* (Nashville: Thomas Nelson Publishers,1992).
2. Robert Bly, *Iron John* (New York: Vintage Books, Random House, Inc.,1990).
3. Ibid.

Chapter three
1. Janice E. Rench, *Family Violence: How to Recognize and Survive It* (Minneapolis: Lerner Publications Company).
2. Mickeal, *A Broken Promise*, self-published.
3. David Johnson and Jeff VanVonderen, *The Subtle Power Of Spiritual Abuse* (Minneapolis: Bethany House Publishers, 1991).
4. Ibid.
5. Ibid.
6. Walter Anderson, *The Confidence Course* (Perennial, 1998).
7. Ibid.
8. Ibid.

Chapter four
1. Wayne W. Dyer, *Manifest Your Destiny* (HarperCollins Pub., Inc., 1997)
2. Ibid.
3. The National Center for PTSD (post-traumatic stress disorder) defines it as psychiatric disorder that can occur following the experience or witnessing of life-threatening events such as military combat, natural disasters, terrorist incidents, serious accidents, abuse (sexual, physical, emotional, ritual), and violent personal assults like rape. It can bring

about marital problems and divorces, family discord, and difficulties in parenting.

4. Becky Mollenkamp, "The Art of Forgiveness" (*Better Homes and Gardens*).

5. Ada Wolf, *A Miracle of Forgiveness*, used with permission from upcoming book.

Chapter five

1. Craig Hill, *The Ancient Paths* (Family Foundations).

2. John DeVriese, *Unexpected Joy* (Grand Rapids, MI: Bibles for India)

Chapter six

1. John Trent, *Choosing to Live The Blessing* (Colorado Springs: Waterbrook Press, 1997).

2. Much of this chapter was adapted from a sermon preached by Pastor Jim Holm, New Hope Church, Salem, Oregon.

Chapter seven

1. Dietrich Bonhoeffer, *Letters and Papers from Prison* (Augsburg Fortress Publishing).

2. Stephen Covey, A. Roger Merrill and Rebecca Merrill, *First Things First* (New York: Simon & Schuster, 1995).

3. William Beausay, *Boys!* (Nashville: Thomas Nelson Publishers, 1994).

Review and Study Guide

1. Dan LeLaCheur, *Generational Legacy*, *Breaking the Curse, Starting the Blessing*, Family Survival Inc., 1994, P.O. Box 2114, Eugene, Oregon 97402.

The Legacy Lives On
A Home of Pain or A Home of Power

WHERE YOU CAN FIND THIS BOOK

This book is available through certain bookstores. If you are unable to obtain it near you. You may write to:

FAMILY SURVIVAL MINISTRIES
P.O. BOX 2114
EUGENE, OREGON 97402

Book Price	$ 11.00 each	Postage Paid
Two to five books	$ 10.00 each	Postage Paid
Six or more	$ 9.00 each	Postage Paid

For Dan LeLaCheur's Book

Generational Legacy
Breaking the Curse, Starting the Blessing

One Book	$10.00 each	includes postage and handling
Two to Five Books	$ 9.00 each	
Three to Six Books	$ 8.00 each	
Study Guide	$ 4.50 each	

Purchase four books—you will receive a free Study Guide

Thousands of people have read this book and have been blessed. They have seen family curses removed as they have confronted their past and found God's healing and blessing.